# FOR

EXTREME SPORTS–CRAZY

# BOYS

# ONLY

# FOR

## EXTREME SPORTS–CRAZY

# BOYS

# ONLY

**JOHN COY**

ILLUSTRATED BY
**HEADCASE DESIGN**

**FEIWEL and FRIENDS**

NEW YORK

A FEIWEL AND FRIENDS BOOK
An Imprint of Macmillan

Feiwel and Friends books may be purchased for business or promotional use. For
information on bulk purchases, please contact the Macmillan Corporate and Premium Sales
Department at (800) 221-7945 x5442 or by e-mail at specialmarkets@macmillan.com.

Library of Congress Cataloging-in-Publication Data
Coy, John, 1958–
For extreme sports-crazy boys only / John Coy ; illustrated by Headcase Design.—First Edition.
pages       cm
Includes bibliographical references.
Audience: Age: 7–12.
ISBN 978-1-250-04944-5 (Hardcover)—ISBN 978-1-250-07862-9 (E-book) 1. Extreme sports—
Juvenile literature. 2. ESPN X-Games—Juvenile literature. 3. Boys—Recreation—Juvenile
literature. I. Headcase Design, ill. II. Title.
GV749.7.C68 2015        796.04'6—dc23        2015013377

Book design by Headcase Design

Feiwel and Friends logo designed by Filomena Tuosto

First Edition: 2015

10 9 8 7 6 5 4 3 2 1

mackids.com

For Alec, Will, and Lizzie,
who go bigger, higher, faster

# CONTENTS

# INTRODUCTION

WE LIKE TO test ourselves. Can I lift this rock? Can I jump over this stream? Can I balance on one foot on this ledge? How far, how fast, how long can I go? Can I push beyond what I think is possible? As long as humans have been on the planet, we've been testing limits and trying to do new things.

For thousands of years, people lived side by side with danger: wild animals, severe weather, difficult terrain, hostile neighbors. How individuals handled fear in the face of danger often determined whether they lived or died.

In the past few decades, however, we've seen a huge emphasis on safety. All kinds of traditional playground equipment such as monkey bars, teeter-totters, and merry-go-rounds have been removed for being too dangerous. Mats and pads have been installed to provide a soft surface for anybody falling. Popular games like king of the hill and dodge-ball have been eliminated for being unsafe.

Teachers, principals, and parents have been trying to make things safer and safer. During the same period we've also seen a huge surge in participation in extreme sports, also known as action sports or adventure sports. And everybody knows that whatever

they're called, these sports are dangerous.

Extreme sports are not a fixed group. They change every day because of the dedication, creativity, and originality of the people who participate in them. This book is an introduction to the wide world of extreme sports. It doesn't cover everything, but it provides a glimpse of what's available and what you might like to explore.

Who knows? Maybe like Alan "Ollie" Gelfand you'll invent a skateboard trick that becomes so important that millions of people will use your nickname as they copy what you created. Who knows? Maybe like David Belle and Sébastien Foucan you'll invent your own extreme sport like they did with parkour and free running. Who knows? Maybe like Shaun White you'll become a gold medal winner in the winter and summer X Games and at the Olympics. Who knows? Maybe you'll be happy hanging out with your friends and supporting one another as you perform tricks you've never done before.

Welcome to the exciting world of extreme sports. Dig in and discover what interests you. And always remember the two words of advice that athletes in these sports offer over and over: Have fun.

# EXPLO

ARE YOU CRAZY about extreme sports? Are you eager to try new ways to go bigger, higher, faster? Are you willing to put in the work to master a new trick and go right on to the next one? Then this book is for you.

Extreme sports have exploded in popularity. Many of them developed as a reaction against traditional sports like baseball, football, basketball, and soccer. Those sports emphasize fitting in and being part of a team with a coach, assistant coaches, uniforms, and structured practices. Instead of following the rules like traditional sports, extreme sports focus on freedom, originality, and creating your own way of doing things.

Parents are much more heavily involved in traditional sports as coaches, spectators, and referees of young athletes. In extreme sports, athletes usually practice away from parents with their concerns and suggestions. Instead of coaches telling them what to do and how to do it, extreme-sport athletes figure out what they

# SION

can do on their own or by talking to friends. Using trial and error and knowing that taking falls is part of the process, they define, refine, and push the limits of what they can do.

These sports are attractive to a much younger age group than traditional sports. The average age of people watching some baseball games is now over sixty. Many extreme-sport athletes are attracted to their sports because they want to be participants, not spectators. Rather than traditional sports that have been around for over 100 years, they want to participate in something new and exciting. They want to create new tricks to amaze themselves and change what everybody else thought was possible.

"I've always been a guy who wants to play sports, not watch them." **—Shaun White, snowboarder and skateboarder**

"No violence, no competition, no groups, no chiefs." **—Sébastien Foucan, free runner**

# EXTREME,

# ADVENTURE,

# ACTION

WHAT'S IN A name? Quite a bit. With its focus on being an individual, taking risks, and testing limits, the term *extreme sports* separated these new sports from other sports. They were more extreme with athletes dealing directly with danger and putting their lives on the line. As these sports grew, the word *extreme* proved attractive to marketers of many products as well.

Over time, some people rebelled against the term *extreme sports*. They objected to *extreme* being used to market sports drinks, shampoo, and deodorant. They objected to their sports being defined in a limited way compared with traditional sports. They didn't like the label *extreme* when they were growing faster and attracting more athletes than sports like baseball.

Some people used the name *adventure sports*, but this too was based on a comparison with traditional sports. The new sports were more adventurous, but *adventure sports* didn't capture the sense of working day after day to perfect a move or develop a new trick. Adventure is an aspect of these sports, but the term *adventure sports* didn't catch on the way some people hoped.

The other term people started using was *action sports*. These new sports do have more action than sports like baseball, but all sports have action. What distinguishes extreme sports from traditional sports is the type of action. And this action is much more extreme when athletes jump out of helicopters onto skateboard ramps, kayak off 70-foot waterfalls, or front-flip 450-pound snowmobiles.

Extreme sports cover a wide range of activities, and many athletes in sports like extreme aerobatics, extreme pogo, and BASE jumping embrace the term. Some athletes in other sports like windsurfing, skateboarding, and snowboarding that have wider acceptance dislike it and prefer to use *action sports*. Or they just refer to their sport as a sport.

We keep circling back to extreme. "Extreme" is what the *X* in X games stands for, and in the absence of a better term for this large, diverse group of sports and the different individuals who participate in them, people continue to call them extreme sports. Perhaps you and your friends will be the ones who come up with a new name that captures the excitement, innovation, and originality of these sports. Perhaps your new name will be what everybody calls them in the future.

For now, we'll use the term *extreme sports*, knowing that it has limitations, even as the people who love these sports test themselves and strive to break the limitations of their sports every single day.

"It's that adrenaline rush I think that comes with extreme sports. For me it's all about the passion of sport and the goodwill that sport creates." **—Robby Naish, windsurfer and kitesurfer**

# TEAM SPORTS

## VERSUS

# EXTREME SPORTS

WHEN YOU TAKE a look at the qualities between these types of sports, what's most appealing to you? What are your priorities in how you spend your time? Both traditional sports and extreme sports have values that they emphasize. There's obviously overlap between them such as hard work, dedication, and the pursuit of excellence. If you're the type of person who values having a coach, being a member of a team, and working within established rules, team sports may be right for you.

If, on the other hand, you value independence, originality, and your own rules, these other sports may be your home. Of course, many kids combine the two and do some of each. But eventually, most people make a choice.

In the matchup between team sports and extreme sports, which would win for you? Who are you and what do you like?

Once you decide, the possibilities are endless.

"For those searching for something more than just the norm. We lay it all down, including what others call sanity, for just a few moments on waves larger than life. We do this because we know there is still something greater than all of us. Something that inspires us spiritually. We start going downhill when we stop taking risks."
**—Laird Hamilton, surfer**

| TEAM SPORTS | EXTREME SPORTS |
| --- | --- |
| Coaches Lead | Athletes Lead |
| Parents as Spectators | Friends as Participants |
| Tryouts to Make the Team | No Tryouts |
| Structured Practice | Unstructured Practice |
| Team Uniforms | Choose Your Own Style |
| Competition for a Starting Spot | Cooperation with Peers |
| Often School Sanctioned | Not Connected with School |
| Following Coach's Instructions | Creating Original Moves |
| Pressure to Win | Emphasis on Having Fun |
| Coach Determines Practice Time | Athlete Determines Practice Time |
| Practice Same Thing Over and Over | Can Practice New Things |
| Coach Decides Who Plays and How Long | Athlete Decides How Long to Play |
| Parents Heavily Involved | Parents Less Involved |
| Emphasis on Statistics | Emphasis on Style |
| Practice Even if You Don't Feel Like It | Practice When You Want |
| Emphasis on Being Part of a Group | Emphasis on Individuality |
| Rules of the Game | Freedom of Expression |
| Emphasis on Tradition | Emphasis on Creativity |
| Team | Individual |

WHAT HAPP

TRADIT

W HEN YOU ASK kids who don't play football, baseball, basketball, or soccer why they don't, one group of people comes up repeatedly: adults. Specifically parents and coaches. Here's a sample of reasons kids give:

"Coaches and parents care too much about winning. If we lose, it's no fun."

"Parents always think they know what you should be doing even if they don't."

"My mom and dad yell from the stands, and it's super embarrassing."

"Practice is so boring. We do the same thing every day."

"My coach has favorites. I'm not one of them, so I don't get to play."

"My dad acts like winning is all that matters."

"Adults put too much pressure on kids to be perfect."

"My mom cares more if we win than I do."

"Coaches think you're not trying even when you are."

"My dad always tells me to have fun, but after the game he tells me what I should have done better no matter what I did."

"It's too much stress."

"I don't get to play enough."

"I'm not going to play in the pros so why does my dad act like my whole future depends on how I do in the game?"

"We sit around waiting for something to happen."

"Coaches don't like players who are too independent."

"I don't need some coach yelling at me all the time."

"It's not fun."

ENED TO

ONAL

SPORTS?

In addition to these reasons, a number of changes have taken place with traditional sports. Many sports now emphasize elite teams that require a huge time commitment for practices and games. Some coaches of elite teams require athletes to specialize and choose one sport above all else. Consequently, many athletes get injured because of overuse of specific muscles related to that sport. Other athletes burn out and lose their enthusiasm at a young age.

Another thing to think about when you're choosing sports is how long you want to participate. Most kids in football never play an official game once they graduate from high school. For most football players, their career ends when they're eighteen. Then they become spectators, rather than participants. Determining how long you want to play is significant in choosing your sports.

One other reason that many kids are turned off by traditional sports is one that adults don't talk about. Some adults want their kids to do better in sports than they did. They do this as a way to live through their kids and feel better about themselves. Some of these adults push their kids way too hard. They stress the importance of winning each game and being the best. They attend games and yell too loudly and are quick to blame umpires and referees. They get too excited over wins and too disappointed over losses. They are too critical of their kids after games. They also are critical of other kids on the team and the manager and coaches. These adults, who get way too involved in the sports their kids play, often don't realize that they're sucking the fun out of it for everybody else.

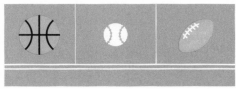

# RISE OF

SOME EXTREME SPORTS like mountain climbing, free diving, and rock climbing have been around for thousands of years. Being able to climb higher and faster provided an advantage for escaping enemies or finding food. Being able to dive deeper and longer on a single breath provided an advantage in searching for valuable pearls or sponges. These sports grew out of things people were doing to survive.

Another source of modern extreme sports is Hawai'i and traditional Polynesian culture. This ancient culture is closely connected with the Pacific Ocean. In addition to being master sailors, Polynesians gave us surfing, which provided the basis for the board sports that followed—on water and on land.

Surfing spread from Hawai'i to California and from California to the rest of the country. Music, television, and films in the 1960s and 1970s used surfing to celebrate youth culture and hanging out at the beach. Surfing styles and techniques had a huge influence on skateboarding since many early skateboarders started as surfers. They used skateboards on land to imitate the moves surfers were making on waves.

In the mid-1970s Southern California suffered through a major drought and severe restrictions were placed on water use. Because of this, some homeowners didn't fill their backyard pools. A few skateboarders realized that these empty pools were ideal places to skate, and they started going higher and higher on the sides. Some even cleared the edge, twisted in the air, and landed back on the side of the pool. These aerials on vertical walls revolutionized skateboarding. It moved it from the ground into the air. It also influenced all the other sports that now emphasize Aerials, Vert, and Big Air.

When looking at the beginnings of different extreme sports, it's striking how many of them took off in the sixties and seventies. The war in Vietnam, the Watergate crisis in government, and the rise of youth culture led to questioning of traditional institutions and ways of doing things. This happened with sports as well. Young people took a new look at traditional sports with coaches, rules, and structured

# EXTREME SPORTS

practices. Many of them decided they wanted something different, something with more emphasis on individuality and originality.

Initially, many of the people who gravitated toward extreme sports thought of themselves as outsiders. They created different ways to participate, dress, and relate to one another. Some of these challenged and angered people in more-established sports. Over time, as the new sports, fashions, and attitudes became more and more popular, the new sports became less alternative and more a part of the culture. This produced arguments among participants about selling out and whether they were losing their outsider edge.

More and more corporations and their advertisers for products such as Red Bull and Mountain Dew wanted to associate them with the new sports to reach a younger audience. The creation of the X Games by ABC and ESPN, part of the Walt Disney Corporation; the Gravity Games by a partnership including NBC; and the Dew Tour, organized by a branch of NBC Sports all were examples of this. Perhaps the biggest indicator of this shift is that the organizers of the Olympics decided they needed new sports to reach a younger audience and added windsurfing, mountain biking, snowboarding, and freestyle skiing.

In 1996, there were 200 skate parks in the United States. Now there are over 3,000. Even with this acceptance of the new sports, there are many athletes who see themselves as outsiders who want to test limits and create something new. These are the athletes who have pushed these sports to the place they are now and these are the athletes who will take them to places we cannot even imagine.

"Skateboarding is as much, or more of, an art or mode of expression than it is a sport. What skateboarding has given me is precisely that: a form of expression that drew me to it, and, in so doing, I was able to express and be who I wanted to be through it, in a sense. And establish myself within a community that were all essentially outsiders like myself. And by doing that, it gave me a place, a sense of belonging." **—Rodney Mullen, skateboarder**

# REASONS TO PARTICIPATE

**K**IDS GIVE LOTS of different reasons when asked why they like to participate in extreme sports.

"It's fun. You can do what you want."

"I get to figure things out without anybody telling me how to do it."

"I get to hang out with my friends."

"I never wanted to be like everybody else."

"Nobody bothers me here."

"When I do something new, people are happy for me."

"It's the best feeling in the world."

"I meet cool people."

"I like practicing new things."

"Friends, fun, and hanging out."

"I want to be able to do something nobody else can do."

"If you work on a trick for a day, you can do it."

"You get to do something you like and get better at it."

"I get away from the house and out with my friends."

"It helps me to let go of my anger. It's a good way to relieve stress."

"It makes everything else in life easier."

"It's challenging. I like working out the problems."

"I like the crashes."

"You're your own coach."

"It's the best, man."

# WHY?

G EORGE MALLORY, THE famous mountain climber, had an answer that became famous when asked why he wanted to climb Mount Everest, the highest mountain on earth.

"Because it's there," Mallory said.

That response indicates the desire of men like Mallory to test themselves in relation to the world around them. Mallory offered other reasons for wanting to climb Mount Everest as well.

"If you cannot understand that there is something in man which responds to the challenge of this mountain and goes out to meet it, that the struggle is the struggle of life itself upward and forever upward, then you won't see why we go," Mallory said. "What we get from this adventure is just sheer joy. And joy is, after all, the end of life. We do not live to eat and make money. We eat and make money to be able to live. That is what life means and what life is for."

Joy. One simple word that captures the feeling of being deeply engaged in a favorite activity. Extreme-sports athletes describe a process where everything from the outside world falls away when they are fully into their sport. They aren't thinking about problems at home or at school. They aren't thinking about issues with other people. They are present, focused, and fully alive.

That feeling is so powerful that people practice over and over to obtain it. Sometimes when watching athletes work on the same trick twenty or thirty times and getting more exhausted, you wonder how they can keep going. When they finally nail it, the feeling of satisfaction, of accomplishment, of joy is powerful. To experience that feeling is why they keep coming back for more.

Duke Kahanamoku, the champion Olympic swimmer and legendary surfer, was central in expanding surfing from Hawai'i to the rest of the country. He was called the "Father of Surfing," and he had a simple way to determine who was the best surfer at a beach.

> "The best surfer out there is the one having the most fun." —Duke Kahanamoku

Nicolas Müller, one of snowboarding's most creative athletes, who largely avoids competitions and specializes in riding difficult terrain, echoes this theme.

> "Snowboarding, that's what it's all about—having fun—and there's nobody who can tell you how you're having the most fun. You've got to find it out for yourself." —Nicolas Müller

Adventure. Joy. Fun. Choose the word that best describes how you feel about your sport and you'll have the answer to the question why.

# 5 QUESTIONS

## FOR ALAN "OLLIE" GELFAND

ALAN GELFAND MOVED from New York to Florida when he was 5 and started skateboarding in 1974 at age 11. Two years later he was a South Florida skateboard champion. Skateboard City, a skateboarding park in Port Orange, Florida, opened in 1976 and Skateboard USA opened in his hometown of Hollywood, Florida, in 1977. Alan is the inventor of the ollie, the trick of pushing the back foot down on the tail of the board to pop the board in the air and using the front foot to level it off. The ollie is the foundation for much of modern skateboarding and other sports.

Alan maintains a Web site that provides articles and pictures from skating's early days: ollieair.com.

He also runs Olliewood, a skating and recreational facility in Hollywood, Florida: olliewood.org

**HOW DID YOU INVENT THE OLLIE?**
Our skateboard parks in Florida were so bumpy when I was starting out and it was a reaction to that. The terrain helped me come up with something new in 1977, and people started calling it the ollie pop, which became the ollie.

**HOW DOES IT FEEL TO HAVE SUCH A MAJOR TRICK NAMED AFTER YOU?**
It's pretty funny. I'm the world's most famous skateboarder that nobody knows.

**WHAT DO YOU THINK OF SKATING TODAY?**
It's great because we had no idea it would get this big. It's much more commercial now. Kids don't realize that people film for a year or two to get a forty-five-minute film. Some kids go out and expect to do things like that right away and get disappointed when they can't.

**ANY ADVICE FOR YOUNG SKATERS?**
Skateboarding is an expression of a person. It's an extension of a person. Skate because you like to skate. Don't do it to impress others. Don't do it to try and get a sponsor. Skate because you love it. It's about joy in doing it for yourself.

**ANYTHING ELSE FOR SKATERS TO THINK ABOUT?**
The people you skate with, many of them will be your friends for life. I've got friends who are doctors, lawyers, scientists, and artists who I became friends with through skating. Skateboarding is about making friends and having fun.

# DANGER

EXTREME SPORTS ARE dangerous. That's one of the reasons we like them. But considering the large number of participants, some of them are substantially safer than traditional sports.

"A Comprehensive Study of Sports Injuries in the United States" by American Sports Data examined different sports and their injury rates. It looked at total participants, injured participants, and the rate of injuries per 100,000 participants. This last category is the best one to compare injury rates between sports. It showed that baseball (5.8), basketball (7.6), soccer (9.3), and football (18.8) players were much more likely to be injured than skateboarders (3.1).

- Baseball players were almost twice as likely to be injured as skateboarders.
- Basketball players were over twice as likely.
- Soccer players were three times as likely.
- And football players were *six* times time more likely to be injured than skateboarders.

All sports have some element of danger, but the injury rates of many extreme sports are below those of most traditional sports. Even activities we think of as safe like walking to the store or riding the bus to school can result in being hurt. How we pay attention to risk and respond to it greatly influences the chances of being injured.

# EMERGENCY ROOM VISITS

T HE AMERICAN ACADEMY of Pediatrics calculates that more than 775,000 children under the age of 14 are treated each year in hospital emergency rooms mainly because of falling, colliding, or being struck by an object. As part of the National SAFE KIDS Campaign, they determined which sports required the most frequent visits to a hospital emergency room for kids aged 5 to 14.

| EMERGENCY ROOM VISITS PER YEAR | |
|---|---|
| Bicycling | 285,000 |
| Basketball | 205,400 |
| Football | 185,700 |
| Baseball and Softball | 108,300 |
| Trampoline | 80,000 |
| Soccer | 75,000 |
| Skateboarding | 50,000 |
| Skiing/Snowboarding | 35,000 |
| Inline Skating | 27,200 |

From these numbers, it's clear that baseball, basketball, football, and soccer still account for the vast majority of emergency room visits by kids. It's also clear that the greatest chance of an ER visit comes from riding your bike. Riding your bike or being driven in a car to practice might be more dangerous than participating in your favorite extreme sport itself.

# EXTREME DANGER

AMONG EXTREME sports, some activities are much more dangerous than others. The sports that involve jumping off buildings, bridges, or mountain cliffs are the most dangerous. The most extreme measure of the danger of a sport is the death rate. While players have died in traditional sports, including 25 high school football players between 2004 and 2013, some extreme sports have much higher rates of death.

A 2012 report from *Extreme Sport News* online listed skydiving and hang gliding as dangerous, but the most dangerous sport by far is BASE jumping and its offshoot, wingsuit flying. BASE stands for Building, Antenna, Span (bridges), and Earth (mountainsides and cliffs). In BASE jumping, participants jump from one of these places and free-fall before deploying their parachutes. In wingsuit flying, participants wear special suits that make them look like flying superheroes and zoom down at speeds in excess of 100 miles an hour before they open their parachutes.

Of the more than 200 BASE jumpers who have died since 1981, almost 100 have died in the past five years since wingsuit flying has become popular. From the summer of 2012 to the summer of 2013, of the 22 BASE jumpers who died, 18 were wearing wingsuits. The super-slow-motion videos of wingsuit flyers are amazing, but these mask the fast speed. Split-second decisions of these flyers can mean the difference between life and death.

"If you're tuned in there's 'Yes.' On the mediocre days, there are two other voices. One's 'Fear.' Your body is screaming out at you, 'Don't do this,' because it's dangerous, unnatural. You're there to conquer your fear. But there's another voice that hangs around every now and again, and that's called 'No.' Something's not right. You can never put your finger on it—it could be something in your pack job, or the weather, or the people you're jumping with, or your mind-set. It's just 'Walk away, don't go jumping today.' The difficulty is trying to discern between 'Fear' and 'No,' because they're both telling you the same thing. 'No' is your sixth sense that's trying to save your life." **—Dave McDonnell, BASE jumper**

YOU CAN TAKE some basic precautions to make participating in extreme sports safer. Most injuries occur when athletes haven't warmed up or are not wearing proper protective gear. Warming up and wearing protective gear will not only help keep you safe, but it will also give you more time to enjoy your sport and less time to sit out because of injuries.

One precaution that many experts offer is don't expect to be able to perform the cool tricks you've seen immediately. "Kids watch extreme-sporting events on television and they think flying through the air on a snowboard looks easy," says Dr. George Russell, spokesperson for the American Academy of Orthopaedic Surgeons (AAOS). "They do not see all the practice it takes to do that—and they don't see how often extreme athletes get injured while learning their stunts."

As part of its Prevent Injuries America! campaign, the AAOS offers tips for athletes participating in winter extreme sports, but many of these apply to all athletes.

- Cold muscles, tendons, and ligaments are more susceptible to injury. Do some light exercise for at least 3 to 5 minutes, then slowly and gently stretch the muscles to be exercised, holding each stretch for at least 30 seconds.

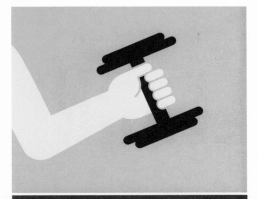

- Do not try to imitate stunts seen in televised events. The people in those events—even the X Games, which appear to be less formal than events like the Olympics—are professional athletes with years of training.

- Never participate in extreme sports alone. Many extreme-sports enthusiasts have a coach or responsible party overseeing any activity. Have a partner who can assist you or go for help if you get injured.

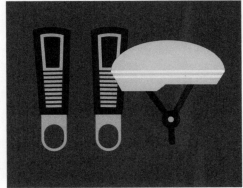

- Wear appropriate protective gear, including goggles, helmets, gloves, and padding, and make sure equipment is in good working order and used properly.

- Take frequent water breaks to prevent dehydration and overheating.

- Avoid participating in any sport when experiencing pain or exhaustion.

- For warmth and protection, wear several layers of light, loose, and water- and wind-resistant clothing. Layering allows you to add and remove clothing to accommodate your body's constantly changing temperature when outside or in a cold environment such as an indoor ice rink.

- Wear proper footwear that provides warmth and dryness, as well as ample ankle support.

- When falling, try to fall on your side or buttocks. Roll over naturally, turning your head in the direction of the roll.

## HOW TO

# LEARN TO FALL

ONE OF THE things that will happen when you participate in extreme sports is you'll fall. As surfer Laird Hamilton puts it, "Wiping out is an underappreciated skill." Learning how to fall so you don't get seriously injured is essential.

## TIPS FOR FALLING

### 1. PROTECT YOUR HEAD.

This is the most important part of your body. You don't want to hit it on a hard surface such as concrete or ice. Get your hands or arms in front of your head to cushion the blow.

### 2. BEND YOUR ANKLES AND KNEES AND CURL INTO YOUR BODY.

This will help minimize chances of hitting your head.

### 3. ROLL AS YOU HIT THE GROUND.

This will distribute the force of impact when falling from a height.

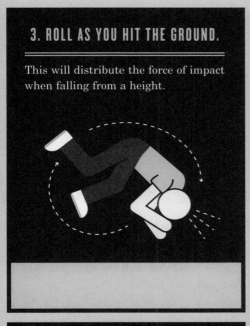

### 4. PRACTICE.

Falling from low heights or on soft surfaces will give you the experience of falling and you can practice protecting yourself in a safe environment.

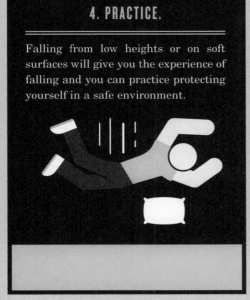

### 5. GET BACK UP AND TRY AGAIN.

Tip 5 will determine what type of athlete you are. Learning how to fall, getting back up, and practicing some more are skills that you will use repeatedly throughout your life.

## ATTITUDE

ONCE YOU'VE CHOSEN your sport or sports, it's up to you to determine how good you want to be. In traditional sports, coaches push players to be better. In extreme sports, the motivation and drive to improve come from the individual. One of the attractions of these sports is that the athlete is responsible for his attitude and his performance. How great do you want to be?

## YOUR BODY

HOW YOU TAKE care of your body will be a major factor in how good you can be. If you are severely injured, you'll lose practice time and it may affect your confidence when you return. Eating well, getting enough sleep, and being focused and alert will all help you perform at your maximum ability. Wearing the right protective gear for your sport will shield you from injuries and provide you with the time you need to improve your skills.

## HARD WORK

THE BIGGEST FACTOR in how good you will be is how hard you work. Malcolm Gladwell in his book *Outliers, The Story of Success* emphasizes the 10,000-hour rule. This rule sets up 10,000 hours as the amount of practice time necessary to master a subject. Gladwell goes through examples from the Beatles to Bill Gates and Steve Jobs to show how putting in 10,000 hours is a significant determiner of future success.

## FAILURE

FOR GREAT ATHLETES, failure is directly connected with success. Rather than getting crushed by disappointment

# GREAT?

when they lose a competition, these athletes go back and practice to get better. They use failure as motivation and an opportunity to figure out what went wrong and how they can make adjustments. As champion BMX rider Mat "The Condor" Hoffman says, "If you want to experience all the successes and pleasures in life, you have to be willing to accept all the pain and failure that comes with it."

## PUTTING IT TOGETHER

IF YOU THINK of the athletes you love, chances are high that they have put their 10,000 hours into practicing and experienced many failures. They use this as fuel to accomplish their goals. This perseverance

is much easier when they are doing what they love. Shaun White loves snowboarding and skateboarding, so working on a trick for days doesn't feel like repetitive work. It's much more a challenge of gravity and physics to overcome, a problem to solve.

## APPLICATION

YOU HAVE THE freedom to determine how great you want to be with your sport. There aren't shortcuts to greatness. It involves having the right attitude, taking care of your body, getting back up when you fall, and putting the hard work into developing your talents. And as Bob Burnquist points out, once you do this in one area, you can transfer this determination, dedication, and effort to other areas in your life.

Bob Burnquist, the legendary skateboarder who has appeared in every summer X Games, says, "What keeps me doing this is freedom. The accomplishments are all mine, no one else's. We have to know we can do things ourselves and not rely on others. There's a whole process of learning a trick that's about growing and character, and you try to transfer that to your life."

# EXCELLENT

| | | |
|---|---|---|
| "The Prince" | Brian Aragon | *Aggressive Inline Skater* |
| "Red Baron" | Éric Barone | *Mountain Biker* |
| "Fearless Felix" | Felix Baumgartner | *Skydiver and BASE Jumper* |
| "Silent Assassin" | Sven Boekhorst | *Aggressive Inline Skater* |
| "Big Bob" | Bob Burnquist | *Skateboarder* |
| "DeG" | Patrick de Gayardon | *Skydiver and Wingsuit Flyer* |
| "The Duke" | Orlando Duque | *Cliff Diver* |
| "Spider-Man" | Sébastien Foucan | *Free Runner* |
| "Ollie" | Alan Gelfand | *Skateboarder* |
| "The Gonz" | Mark Gonzales | *Skateboarder* |
| "The Birdman" | Tony Hawk | *Skateboarder* |
| "The Condor" | Mat Hoffman | *Freestyle BMX Rider* |
| "Murda" | Mike Johnson | *Aggressive Inline Skater* |
| "The Jeweler" | Jacob Juul | *Aggressive Inline Skater* |
| "Father of Surfing" | Duke Kahanamoku | *Surfer* |
| "Uncle K" | Kealoha Kaio | *Surfer* |
| "Sketchy Andy" | Andy Lewis | *Slackliner* |

# NICKNAMES

| | | |
|---|---|---|
| "da Rippa" | Jack Lindholm | *Bodyboarder* |
| "Bam" | Brandon Margera | *Skateboarder* |
| "Whitesnake" | Joey Marks | *BMX Rider* |
| "The Godfather" | Mike Metzger | *Freestyle Moto X Rider* |
| "Miracle Boy" | Dave Mirra | *BMX Rider* |
| "Yuck Yuckem" | Franky Morales | *Aggressive Inline Skater* |
| "Palm Daddy" | Shaun Palmer | *Snowboarder* |
| "iPod" | Iouri Podladtchikov | *Snowboarder* |
| "Nugget" | Nathan Purcell | *Bodyboarder* |
| "P-Rod" | Paul Rodriguez | *Skateboarder* |
| "Monster Mike" | Mike Schultz | *Snowmobiler* |
| "The Swiss Machine" | Ueli Steck | *Mountain Climber* |
| "Twitch" | Jeremy Stenberg | *Freestyle Moto X Rider* |
| "Wingnut" | Robert Weaver | *Surfer* |
| "The Flying Tomato" | Shaun White | *Snowboarder and Skateboarder* |
| "The Jailer" | Jake Windham | *Freestyle Moto X Rider* |

# BASIC SKATE

- **AIR:** amount of space created by riding with all four wheels off the ground

- **BACKSIDE:** a trick executed with the skater's back to the ramp or obstacle

- **BOARDSLIDE:** to slide the underside of the deck along an object

- **BRAIN BUCKET:** a helmet

- **CABALLERIAL:** a 360-degree turn on a ramp while riding fakie (backward), named after Steve Caballero

- **CARVE:** to skate in a long, curving arc

- **DECK:** the actual board, usually made from laminated maple

- **DROP-IN:** to put the tail of the board on the coping of a ramp and step on the front of the board to enter the ramp

- **FACE PLANT:** a landing on the face before any other part of the body

- **FAKIE:** rolling backward on the board

- **FRONTSIDE:** trick executed with the skater facing the ramp or obstacle

- **FS 540:** a frontside 540-degree turn

- **GRAB:** to grab the board with one or both hands

- **GRIND:** to scrape one or both trucks on a curb, railing, or other surface

  - **50-50 Grind:** a grind on both trucks

  - **5-0 Grind:** a rear-truck grind with the front of the board elevated

  - **Nosegrind:** a front-truck grind with the rear of the board elevated

- **HALFPIPE:** a ramp shaped like a U and used for vert skating

- **HARD FLIP:** (instead of the board spinning backside) a trick performed by doing a kickflip and having the board spin frontside

- **HEELFLIP:** a kickflip in which the skater uses the front heel to flip the board in the opposite direction

- **INWARD HEELFLIP:** a heelflip variation where the board simultaneously rotates 180-degree backside

- **JUMP RAMP:** a small ramp used to get air to perform tricks

- **KICKFLIP:** an ollie in which the front foot kicks the board into a 360-degree spiral before landing back on it

- **KICK TURN:** a turn made by applying pressure to the tail of the board in order to lift the front

# TERMS

THAT ALSO APPLY TO OTHER SPORTS

- **KNEE SLIDE:** a way to control a fall by sliding on the plastic caps of the knee pads

- **LASER FLIP:** a frontside 360-degree shove-it and a heelflip in which the board does two full rotations

- **LID:** a helmet

- **MANUAL:** the front wheels of the board are lifted off the ground while rolling

- **McTWIST:** a backside 540-degree turn usually attempted on a ramp (named after Mike McGill)

- **MONGO-FOOT:** a push made with the trailing foot kept on the board; most commonly used to push fakie

- **NOLLIE:** a nose ollie; an ollie performed by tapping the nose of the board with the front foot

- **NOSE:** the front of the board

- **NOSE MANUAL:** the back wheels of the board are lifted off the ground while rolling

- **NOSESLIDE:** to slide the underside of the nose of the board on a ledge, rail, or lip

- **OLLIE:** a jump performed by popping the tail of the board on the ground, and using the front foot to even it out in the air

- **POP:** to strike the tail of the board against the ground to propel the board upward

- **POP SHOVE-IT:** a shove-it performed while popping the tail to make the board attain air

- **QUARTERPIPE:** one wall of a halfpipe; a banked jump

- **RAILSLIDE:** a trick in which the underside of the deck slides along an object, such as a curb or handrail

- **SHOVE-IT:** to spin the board 180 degrees beneath the feet without the skater spinning

- **TAILSLIDE:** a trick in which the underside of the tail end of a board slides on a ledge or lip

- **TRUCKS:** the two axle assemblies that connect the wheels to the deck

- **VARIAL HEELFLIP:** same as a hard flip, but the skater heel flips and the board spins front side

- **VARIAL KICKFLIP:** a trick consisting of a backside pop shove-it and a kickflip

- **VERT RAMP:** a halfpipe with steep sides that are vertical near the top

# THE TOP 40

## EXTREME

## SPORTS

AGGRESSIVE INLINE SKATING
TO WINGSUIT FLYING

ENTHUSIASM FOR DIFFERENT extreme sports has risen and fallen over the years. Some that were popular twenty years ago like aggressive inline skating or sky surfing are less popular now. Newer ones like stand up paddle surfing or wingsuit flying have generated lots of interest. There are also the very new sports that most people haven't heard of like extreme pogo. It's difficult to know which of these will take off and which won't stand the test of time.

Making any Top 40 list is a challenge. It's tough to decide which sports to include and which to leave out, as people argue about this frequently. The following list includes forty extreme sports that are receiving lots of attention and have a large number of participants. A brief description of the sport is provided along with its beginnings and some information that may be new to you. As you page through the list, think about which other sports should be included and which you'd leave out to make your own Top 40.

This is not an in-depth exploration of any one sport, but by providing an overview, you can discover sports you didn't know existed and decide which ones you want to know more about. Magazines, books, DVDs, Web sites, and online videos all provide ways to learn more about these sports and anything else that's interesting to you. Have fun!

# AGGRESSIVE
# INLINE
# SKATING

is a form of skating that focuses on jumps, turns, spins, and grinding.

**AKA** blading, powerblading, skating, or rolling

# BEGINNINGS

I N 1980, MINNESOTANS Scott and Brennan Olson started Ole's Innovative Sports, which later became Rollerblade, to provide ice hockey players with a new way to practice in the summer. They developed skates with four polyurethane wheels in a line on the bottom.

Aggressive inline skating became popular in the 1990s after the introduction of tougher inline skates. These allowed riders to grind, sliding on the bottom of the skates.

In 2009, the skaters Brian Shima, Jon Julio, and Kato Mateu created the World Rolling Series. WRS conducts amateur and professional competitions around the world and works to increase the size, recognition, and strength of the sport.

# SKATES

T HESE CAN BE customized and skaters choose different ones for speed versus grinding.

# STYLES

## PARK

Using ramps in a skate park, skaters perform tricks in the air and string together a series of these called "a line."

## STREET

Using rails, ledges, stairs, and other structures of the city, riders attempt grinds, jumps, and other moves on available surfaces.

# EARLY STAR

M IKE "MURDA" JOHNSON developed a successful skating career that took him to events around the world. Now retired from competition, he creates computer graphics and video effects for movies. He taught himself this while reading and experimenting during breaks on skating tours.

"I've traveled to so many places, learned so much, and met so many good friends. It's made me evolve as a person. Had I not skated, I wouldn't be the man I am today."

—Mike "Murda" Johnson

# BASE JUMPING

involves jumping from a fixed object and free-falling before opening a parachute.

## BEGINNINGS

FREDERICK LAW JUMPED from the Statue of Liberty in 1912 using a parachute and landed safely.

Owen Quinn made a jump from the south tower of New York World Trade Center in 1975 to call attention to the number of people who were unemployed.

Carl Boenish popularized modern BASE jumping at El Capitan in Yosemite National Park in 1978. Phil Smith, Phil Mayfield, Jean Boenish, and Carl Boenish became the first four people to jump from all four BASE objects in 1981.

## WHAT "BASE" STANDS FOR

• Building
• Antenna (such as a radio or TV tower)
• Span (such as a bridge or arch)
• Earth (a natural feature such as a cliff or mountain)

## PARACHUTES

BASE-JUMPING PARACHUTES are designed to open faster at lower airspeeds than regular ones. Jumpers don't pack a reserve parachute since there wouldn't be time to open it.

## SUPER JUMP

IN MAY 2008, Dave McDonnell and Hervé le Gallou snuck past security and climbed stairs for one hour and fifteen minutes to reach the 160th floor of the Burj Khalifa in Dubai, the tallest building on Earth. They walked down a few floors to avoid detection, waited a couple of hours until dawn, and then jumped. Le Gallou went back two days later for another attempt and was arrested. He was held in jail for three months before paying a fine and being released.

## RISK

BASE JUMPING AND its offshoot wingsuit flying are the most dangerous extreme sports. So many BASE jumpers have died that it's illegal in many places. Carl Boenish, the modern founder, was the first BASE jumper listed in the Guinness Book of World Records for his jump in 1984 at Trollveggen in Norway. He died making another jump from a slightly higher spot nearby two days later.

"I don't like to sugarcoat things and it's a guarantee that if you get into BASE jumping, you're going to hurt yourself. You're going to break bones. You are going to see people die, and guess what? Some of them are going to be your very good friends. And if you keep BASE jumping long enough, it will kill you." —**Jeb Corliss, BASE jumper**

# BODY-BOARDING

uses a short, rectangular piece of foam on ocean waves. Riders perform backflips, front flips, rolls, and other tricks.

**AKA** boogie boarding

# BEGINNINGS

FOR HUNDREDS OF years, Polynesian people rode alaia boards either by lying flat on the belly or kneeling on them.

Tom Morey went to the beach one day in Hawai'i in 1971, but he didn't have a surfboard. Using a piece of polyethylene foam, a hot iron, and an electric knife, he created the first modern bodyboard. When he tried it, he loved it. "I could actually feel the waves through the board. It was like nothing I'd experienced before."

From its founding in Hawai'i, bodyboarding has grown into a worldwide sport that's popular in Australia, Brazil, Chile, France, New Zealand, Japan, Spain, South Africa, and the United States.

# THREE STYLES OF RIDING

## DROPKNEE
Having one leg forward with the back knee on the board

## PRONE
Lying flat on the board

## STAND UP
Standing up with both feet on the board

# GEAR

- bodyboard and leash to hang on to when your board gets away
- wet suit
- pair of fins
- pair of fin socks

# EARLY STAR

MIKE STEWART OF Hawai'i became interested in bodyboards and talked to Tom Morey about his invention. Stewart dedicated himself to the sport and became a nine-time world champion who had a major influence on later bodyboarders. Today he designs and sells his own line of bodyboards.

# STAR

JEFF HUBBARD FROM Hawai'i is a three-time world champion who's known for spectacular moves in the air. He and his brother Dave created Hubboards, to promote their own bodyboards. Jeff is also active in speaking to kids about finding their passion and following their dreams.

# BUNGEE JUMPING

consists of jumping from a tall structure while attached to an elastic cord. The jumper free-falls until he's pulled back by the cord and ends up at rest in a suspended position.

## BEGINNINGS

REPORTS EXIST OF men diving off of wooden platforms with vines attached to their ankles as a test of courage in the Pentecost Island, Vanuatu, in the South Pacific.

On April 1, 1979, members of the Oxford University Dangerous Sports Club gathered at the Clifton Suspension Bridge in Bristol, England. They bungee jumped from the bridge and the modern sport was born. Members of the group were arrested but news of bungee jumping spread.

## SCENIC SPOTS

- Royal Gorge Bridge in Colorado above the Arkansas River
- The Macau Tower in Macau, China
- Perrine Bridge in Idaho above the Snake River
- Bloukrans Bridge in South Africa
- Verzasca Dam in Ticino, Switzerland, featured in the James Bond movie *GoldenEye*
- Victoria Falls Bridge on the border of Zimbabwe and Zambia

## GOING HIGHER

JOHN KOCKELMAN BUNGEE jumped 2,200 feet from a hot air balloon in California, and Andrew Salisbury jumped 3,157 feet from a helicopter in Mexico.

## CLOSE CALL

IN JANUARY 2012, Erin Langworthy, 22, of Perth, Australia, bungee jumped at the Victoria Falls Bridge on the Zambezi River, a river known to have crocodiles in it. The bungee cord broke and she was plunged into the water with her ankles bound together. She managed to swim to the shore and coughed up water and blood. She suffered a fractured collarbone and body bruises but recovered from her injuries after a week in a South African hospital. Video of her close call is available online.

## RISKS

EVEN THOUGH THOUSANDS of people have successfully bungee jumped, it's still a dangerous sport. That's why jumpers sign a release form stating that they are aware of the possibility of accident, even death. The greatest risk is equipment failure, but others include vision impairment, whiplash, and an increased chance of stroke.

# CAVE DIVING

is a form of technical diving using scuba equipment to explore caves. Scuba, which stands for Self-Contained Underwater Breathing Apparatus, provides air for the diver, allowing him freedom of movement underwater.

## BEGINNINGS

A S LONG AS humans have known about underwater caves, divers have been eager to explore them.

With the introduction of modern scuba-diving equipment in the twentieth century, divers could travel farther and deeper.

## DRAWS

C AVE DIVING OFFERS experienced divers the chance to explore undiscovered places and to work closely with fellow divers while knowing that a mistake or miscalculation could be fatal.

## GEAR

- fins
- mask
- lights
- dry suit or wet suit, depending on the temperature and the length of the dive

## SPECIAL CHALLENGES

- Divers swim facedown and try not to disturb any sediment to keep the water clear.

- The extreme darkness of caves requires special lights.
- Caves may contain unpredictable currents and changes in water level.
- Divers use guidelines in order to find their way back to the cave opening.
- Since it's not possible to shoot straight back to the surface, divers must make sure they have adequate air for the return journey.

## RULE OF THIRDS

- one-third of air for going into the cave
- one-third of air for going out of the cave
- one-third of air in case of emergency, delayed exit, or to support another diver

## CAVERN DIVES VERSUS CAVE DIVES

C AVERN DIVES USE natural light and take place near open water.

Cave dives require artificial light since they move beyond the cavern and into the constant dark of the cave.

"Buoyed by the water, he can fly in any direction—up, down, sideways—by merely flipping his hand. Underwater, man becomes an archangel." **—Jacques Cousteau, pioneer diver**

# CLIFF DIVING

consists of diving from a high cliff, platform, or tower into open water. While free-falling, divers twist, flip, and roll before entering the water.

# BEGINNINGS

PEOPLE HAVE BEEN diving off cliffs into open water for thousands of years, well before historical records were kept.

In 1770, King Kahekili of Maui dove from Kaunolu, a 63-foot cliff, and entered the water cleanly.

In the 1950s, cliff divers in Acapulco, Mexico, became a popular tourist attraction as they dove from over 80 feet into the Pacific Ocean.

# GEAR

CLIFF DIVING IS perhaps the least complicated extreme sport since it requires no special clothing or equipment.

# TOP DIVING SITES

- Acapulco, Mexico
- Brontallo, Switzerland
- Kimberley, Australia
- South Point Cliffs, Hawai'i
- West End Cliffs, Negril, Jamaica

# DIVING STARS

- Orlando Duque, Colombia, nine-time world champion
- Gary Hunt, United Kingdom, three-time world champion and developer of the triple quad, three somersaults and four twists in the same dive
- David Colturi, United States
- Jonathan Paredes, Mexico
- Steven LoBue, United States

# SUPER HIGH DIVE

DAVE KUNZE OF the United States holds the record for the highest uninjured dive of 172 feet. Others, like Olivier Favre of France and Randy Dickison of the United States, have attempted higher dives but were injured in the process.

"I think that the feeling of fear is important for me, because it keeps me focused, it keeps me going through the right steps. I have to go through step one, then step two, then step three to have a good dive. So it helps me get focused to have a more successful dive."

—Orlando Duque

# EXTREME
## AEROBATICS

involves flying specially built aircraft to perform precise maneuvers. The pilot executes rolls, spins, loops, sequences, and low-altitude flying.

## BEGINNINGS

IN 1910, WILBUR and Orville Wright hired a group of professional pilots to perform stunts to draw attention to their new invention, the airplane. This team was called the Wright Fliers.

After World War II, a shortage of jobs and a surplus of airplanes and men who knew how to fly them created ideal conditions for barnstorming stunt pilots.

One of these groups, the Thrasher Brothers Aerial Circus, consisted of Grady, Bud, and Tunis Thrasher of Elberton, Georgia. They developed "The World's Smallest Airport," the back of a moving car with a wooden platform, from which they took off and landed their plane.

## SPECIAL PLANES

- Aerobatic aircraft are stronger than aircraft designed to make long flights.
- They contain quick-escape doors for emergencies.
- They also have special fuel and oil systems that allow for upside-down flying.

## NOT JUST PLANES

CERTAIN HELICOPTERS MAY also be used for aerobatics. Chuck Aaron and the Red Bull team of the United States, the Blue Eagles and Black Cats of the United Kingdom, the Sarang of India, the Scorpions of Poland, the Rotores of Portugal, and the Patrulla Aspa of Spain all specialize in aerobatic helicopter maneuvers.

## STAR

ZOLTÁN VERES OF Hungary holds five Guinness Book of World's Records for aerobatics, including making 408 continuous rolls with his aircraft. He also specializes in low-altitude flying, including flying under bridges. Some of these videos from his Web site are amazing.

"I want to inspire young kids to think outside the box, come up with new computer systems to make it work better or new aerodynamics to make the helicopter fly better. I've done a bit of it and I'm hoping this is inspiring others to do that, too. I want kids not to think it's at the end of the rope. There's plenty more out there that can be dreamed up. Just get out there and do it." **—Chuck Aaron**

# EXTREME POGO

uses special pogo sticks that can bounce up to ten feet high on which athletes perform a variety of tricks.

AKA **Xpogo**

# BEGINNINGS

**M**ANY PEOPLE PERFORMED tricks on conventional steel-sprung pogo sticks. But in 2004, with the invention of the extreme pogo stick, jumpers were able to get much more air, which opened up a new array of tricks.

Dave Armstrong of Provo, Utah, is often credited with popularizing extreme pogo through Xpogo.com, the Web site he created.

# RECORDS

## HIGHEST JUMP ON A POGO STICK

9 feet, 8 inches by Dmitry Arsenyev in Montpellier, France, on May 31, 2014

## HIGHEST BACKFLIP ON A POGO STICK

9 feet, 3 inches by Curt Markwardt in Costa Mesa, California, on July 26, 2012

## HIGHEST FRONT FLIP ON A POGO STICK

9 feet, by Biff Hutchison, Dalton Smith, and Michael Mena in Pittsburgh, Pennsylvania, on July 2, 2014

## MOST CONSECUTIVE FRONT FLIPS ON A POGO STICK

5 by Jake Gartland in Costa Mesa, California, on July 28, 2011

## MOST CONSECUTIVE BACKFLIPS ON A POGO STICK

17 by Fred Grzybowski in Tokyo, Japan, in December 2013

## FARTHEST DISTANCE BOUNCED IN 24 HOURS

26.2 miles by Jack Sexty in Manchester, England, on April 6, 2014

# IT'S UP TO YOU

**X**POGO IS A relatively new sport and records fall quickly. The above records may have been broken by the time you read this. Maybe you'll be the one to go out and set the new mark.

# EVENT

**P**OGOPALOOZA IS AN annual Xpogo event that draws thousands of fans as athletes try to break records and compete for prizes and medals in Big Air, Best Trick, and High Jump.

# FREEDIVING

involves divers taking a breath and then holding it as they go underwater. Divers try to go as deep as possible or stay below as long as they can.

# BEGINNINGS

FOR CENTURIES, PEARL divers, spear fishers, and sponge divers held their breath as they swam underwater. By staying beneath the surface longer, they increased their chances of success.

Today, divers push the boundaries of how deep they can go and how long they can remain underwater. As their heart rates slow, many experience feelings of calm, quiet, and relaxation.

Some divers use weighted sleds to pull them down to maximum depths and inflatable bags to return to the surface.

# FILMS FEATURING FREEDIVING

- *The Big Blue*
- *The Freediver*
- *Into the Blue*
- *Phoenix Blue*
- *You Only Live Twice*

# DANGERS

HOLDING ONE'S BREATH underwater comes with obvious dangers. The body undergoes significant changes when it does not get fresh oxygen.
- The heart rate drops.
- Blood vessels shrink and blood is directed toward the main organs.
- Blood plasma fills up parts of the lungs so they won't collapse.

# DEATH

FREEDIVING CAN BE a dangerous activity and hundreds of divers have died from going too deep, staying underwater too long, or coming up too quickly and getting decompression sickness, commonly known as "the bends."

# PRECAUTIONS

- Always dive under the supervision of a buddy.
- Don't go deeper if you feel pressure on your eardrums.
- If you encounter problems, return to the surface.

"The scuba diver dives to look around. The freediver dives to look inside."

**—Umberto Pelizzari, freediver**

# FREEFLYING

is a form of skydiving in which divers use airflow to perform flips and rolls. They often produce sequences that are filmed by another freeflyer.

# BEGINNINGS

IN 1992, OLAV Zipser founded the FreeFly Clowns with Mike Vail and went on to open a school to teach freeflying, The First School of Modern SkyFlying.

In 1998, freeflying was an exhibition sport at the ESPN X Games. In 2000, the International Parachuting Commission made freeflying an official event with three-person teams, one of whom was a videographer.

# FREEFLYING POSITIONS

## BACK FLYING

This is the opposite of the basic belly-flying position of traditional skydiving and involves looking up to the sky instead of down to the earth. Like the belly position, back flying provides a wide surface area to slow the descent rate.

## SIT-FLY

This basic head-up position is like sitting in a chair with no chair and the wind rushing at you. The goal is to have a ninety degree angle of thighs to hips and lower legs to thighs. It's important to have a straight back, to extend the arms, and to push the feet down against the air pressure.

## STANDING

In this head-up position the legs are pressed down and the speed increases.

Extending the arms will slow the speed by providing more wind resistance.

## HEAD DOWN

The head is down and the feet are up like in a headstand. The legs provide the balance and moving them can increase or decrease speed.

# OLAV ZIPSER'S FIVE STEPS TO FREEFLY SAFETY

1. Eye Contact
2. Level Control
3. Distance Control
4. Breathing/Thinking
5. Communication

# RECORD

THE LARGEST HEAD-DOWN group formation was held on August 4, 2012, when 138 freeflyers linked together at Skydive Chicago. Videos of this include some people playing rock, paper, scissors as they free-fall.

"Freeflying is the art of maneuvering in the sky in every possible way, direction, rotation and speed in control, and with anticipation of the next move." —Olav Zipser

# FREE RUNNING

uses jumps, spins, and acrobatics to move from one point to another, emphasizing self-expression.

# BEGINNINGS

**I**N THE 2003 documentary *Jump London*, three athletes, Sébastien Foucan, Jérome Ben Aoues, and Johann Vigroux, ran, jumped, and leaped around London.

At first, free running was used as an English translation of parkour, the French training method in which participants move around obstacles to get from one point to another as quickly as possible.

Free running, under the leadership of Sébastien Foucan, began to emerge as its own sport with an emphasis on originality and creativity. Foucan said, "Now people recognize parkour with flips as free running, but only the action of doing parkour and flips is not free running. It's the action of adding more stuff into your expression. That's the free-running attitude."

# SÉBASTIEN FOUCAN'S CORE VALUES OF FREE RUNNING

- Follow your way.
- Always practice.
- Respect others in their practice.
- Be an inspiration for others.
- Be positive and look for positive environments.
- Respect your environment.
- Feel free to try other disciplines.
- Don't take it too seriously.

- The journey is more important than the goal.
- There is no good or bad, right or wrong, but what is important is what you learn from experiences through practice.
- Free running is not an elite discipline but for people who love and continue to move.
- Channel your energy in a good way, a way to be better.

"The way is the path of silence. Cut across town quietly at your own speed. Concentrate on footwork, your touch, your own sensibility. Look for catlike silence and you will find the path. This is the way."
**—Sébastien Foucan**

# FREESKIING

is a form of skiing that
emphasizes long, steep descents
outside established trails.
Freeskiers also pull off flips,
grabs, and spins while in the air.

# BEGINNINGS

IN THE 1930s, Norwegian skiers began using acrobatics as part of their training program.

In the 1960s, freestyle skiing, called "hot dog skiing," became popular at ski resorts as skiers pushed the boundaries of the sport, including making longer and steeper descents.

In the 1990s, skiers began to sneak into terrain parks, which at the time were reserved for snowboarders. With the availability of twin-tip skis in the late nineties, new possibilities for freeskiing opened up.

In the 2000s, freeskiing emerged as its own sport with stars such as Shane McConkey who pushed the limits by combining it with BASE jumping before his death in an accident in 2009.

# STYLES

## BACKCOUNTRY

This is the most dangerous form of skiing because of the extreme speeds, large drops, unfamiliar terrain, and the possibility of avalanches.

## PARK

Using jumps and halfpipes, skiers try to get as much air as possible in order to demonstrate flips, grabs, and spins. Many ski parks now have rails and boxes so freeskiers can grind and perform other tricks.

# OLYMPICS

FREESTYLE SKIING BECAME part of the Winter Olympics when moguls became a medal sport in 1992 and aerials in 1994. Halfpipe and slopestyle were added in 2014 after they had been part of the X Games since 2002.

# DANGER

WITH THE RISE of backcountry skiing, runs have become much more dangerous. In response, *Powder* magazine ran a 2012 cover story "Why Are So Many of the Best Young Skiers Dying?"

"What we were doing was free from skiing, free of rules and most any kind of boundaries. Whether it was steep, extreme descents, or new freestyle, what we were doing was freeskiing, free to ski in our own style on our own terms."

**—Shane McConkey**

# FREESTYLE BMX

stands for freestyle bicycle motocross and includes riders demonstrating jumps and tricks on a variety of terrain and surfaces.

# BEGINNINGS

I N THE 1970s, kids in Southern California began riding bikes and creating tricks in empty swimming pools and dry concrete reservoir channels.

In the 1980s, freestyle BMX exploded in popularity with magazines, movies, and television shows featuring riders. New equipment and bikes flowed on to the market and contests and competitions expanded.

# STYLES

## FLATLAND

Riders use smooth surfaces like parking lots or basketball courts to develop tricks that include spinning and balancing on their bikes.

## PARK

In skate parks with concrete or wooden ramps, riders string together a series of tricks in the air.

## TRAILS

Riders zoom around a course of compacted dirt and execute tricks in the air as they fly over jumps.

## VERT

With two quarterpipes facing each other, riders race down one side and up the other, trying to get as much air as possible. Once airborne, they grab different parts of the bike while removing as much of their body from it as possible.

# FOUR BASIC TRICKS

## BUNNY HOP

Jumping the bike in the air from flat ground

## ENDO

Lifting the back wheel using the front brake and balancing on the front tire

## WHEELIE

Lifting the front wheel off the ground while riding on the back wheel

## MANUAL

A wheelie without pedaling

# INCREDIBLE STREAK

B MX SUPERSTAR DAVE MIRRA won at least one medal in every X Games from 1995, when they started, until 2008. During that time, he won more X Games medals than anybody else.

"Hopefully somewhere along the line, I can motivate somebody to be whatever they want to be in life. I feel like that's my whole mission to just psych people to believe in themselves." —**Rick Thorne**

# FREESTYLE
# SCOOTERING

**consists of riders on scooters performing freestyle tricks.**

**AKA scooting, scooter, or scooter riding**

# BEGINNINGS

SCOOTERS HAVE BEEN around for over 100 years and riders invented different moves for them. It was not until the late 1990s, however, that advances in technology produced models that were both stronger and lighter. This allowed freestyle scootering to take off.

# STYLES

## FLATLAND
Using driveways or parking lots, riders put together a series of tricks called a combo that can feature spinning the bars in barspins and rotating the deck in tailwhips.

## PARK
Riders at skate parks use rails, boxes, and vertical ramps for a wide variety of tricks.

## STREET
Using stairs, ledges, rails, and speed bumps, riders improvise tricks based on what's available in the environment.

# RECORD

DAKOTA "KOTA" SCHUETZ holds the record for most kick scooter backflips in one minute with 15.

# CRASHES

EVERY EXTREME SPORT has crashes and freestyle scootering has two that have been viewed repeatedly online.

## 16-STAIR FALL
In 2011, Tom Kvilhaug crashed after jumping 16 stairs when his bars snapped off. He wasn't wearing a helmet and his head hit the ground. Tom's friends called 911 right away and paramedics took him to the hospital. He broke his eye socket and one facial bone and required seven stitches in his left eyebrow. He stayed overnight and was back on his scooter after a couple of weeks.

## 18-FOOT VERT WALL CRASH
In 2007, longtime scooter rider, KC Corning, suffered what he describes as the fall of his life. He tried to drop in on an 18-foot vert wall and face-planted on a concrete floor. He was wearing a helmet and was able to get up from the fall. He recovered, resumed riding, and founded TSI, one of the first rider-owner scooter companies.

"I always wanted scooters to be the cool thing to do so that I wasn't the only one doing it. Now, I go to skate parks sometimes and there are more scooter riders than skateboarders and bikers combined, which is way cool!"

**—KC Corning**

# HANG GLIDING

involves flying in light, nonmotorized aircraft with a fixed-frame body while secured by a harness. Pilots can reach speeds of up to 80 miles per hour and depending on wind conditions can perform loops, spins, or rollovers and fly long distances.

## BEGINNINGS

FOR AS LONG as humans have watched birds, they've dreamed of flying.

In the 1890s, Otto Lilienthal of Germany developed gliders that were controlled by the pilot hanging on to a bar and shifting his weight, the same principle in use today. Lilienthal documented work in a scientific manner and had such an influence that he became known as the Glider King.

## HOW TO FLY

A GLIDER IS heavier than air so it will naturally descend. To counteract this and glide long distances, pilots must find rising warm air masses called thermals. Pilots use their own observations and a variometer, a vertical speed indicator, to identify thermals and circle within the rising air.

## JUST IN CASE

PILOTS CARRY A parachute enclosed in the harness in case they need to make an emergency landing.

## RECORD GLIDE

ON JULY 3, 2012, Dustin Martin and Jonny Durand set out from Zapata, Texas, hoping to break the world record for distance. They didn't realize when they started how ideal the conditions were, but as they soared over the Texas countryside, each knew they had a shot at breaking the old record of 438 miles. When they crossed that mark late in the day, they knew that whoever went farther would have the new record. They both tried to hang on as the sun began to set and the winds died down. Dustin Martin edged out Jonny Durand and landed just outside of Lorenzo, Texas. His flight took 11 hours and covered 475 miles, roughly the distance from New York City to Detroit.

"For once you have tasted flight you will walk the earth with your eyes turned skywards, for there you have been and there you will long to return." **—Leonardo da Vinci**

# ICE CLIMBING

consists of climbing ice formations such as icefalls, ice cliffs, or frozen waterfalls using an ice ax, boots with crampons, ropes, and ice screws.

# BEGINNINGS

PEOPLE HAVE BEEN climbing ice for thousands of years. In recent years, technological advances have produced better equipment that has led to climbers undertaking more difficult climbs.

# DANGERS

IN ADDITION TO the challenges of razor-sharp ice axes and crampons, ice climbers face the dangers of crevasses, avalanches, and falling ice.

# TYPES OF ICE

### ALPINE ICE
Ice in the mountains that is frozen solid

### WATER ICE
Ice that has water flowing underneath it and that flows freely in the summer

# ICE GRADING

ICE CLIMBING MAINTAINS a system of grading to determine the difficulty of specific climbs, but since ice conditions change based on weather and previous climbers, there is always a degree of subjectivity involved.

# RECORD

FROM NOON ON January 9, 2013, to noon on January 10, 2013, Will Gadd attempted to set the record for longest continual ice climb at Ouray Ice Park in Ouray, Colorado. He climbed for 24 hours and recorded 194 laps, a total distance of 25,414 feet, higher than the elevation of Mount McKinley, the highest mountain in North America. He set this record while raising over $15,000 for dZi, an organization that works on community development in Nepal.

"No matter how many times or what I've climbed, it always strikes me as unlikely when I step off the ground that it actually works. If you think about it, it's just like climbing a hockey rink standing on its end." —**Will Gadd**

# KITESURFING

**uses the wind to propel a kite that pulls a kitesurfer on a board across the surface of water and into the air for jumps, spins, and flips.**

AKA **kiteboarding, kiting**

## BEGINNINGS

IN 1902, SAMUEL Cody, an American inventor and showman, built a kite that pulled a boat across the English Channel.

Two French brothers, Dominique and Bruno Legaignoux, developed an inflatable kite design in the 1970s that opened the way for new advances.

In the 1990s, led by innovations in design by Bill and Cory Roeseler in the United States, kitesurfing took off.

## STORM CHASERS

ELITE KITESURFERS STUDY weather and wind patterns in order to get maximum air. This leads some of them to search out storms and go out in extremely strong winds. Videos of kitesurfers in these conditions provide a sense of how intense this sport can be.

## STARS

- Jesse Richman, United States
- Sam Light, United Kingdom
- Nick Jacobsen, Denmark
- Gianni Aragno, Spain
- Lewis Crathern, United Kingdom
- Rick Jensen, Germany
- Youri Zoon, the Netherlands
- Remi Muen, Norway
- Ruben Lenten, the Netherlands

## LONG-DISTANCE RECORD

IN A 24-HOUR period from May 10 to May 11, 2010, Philip McCoy Midler kitesurfed from South Padre Island, Texas, to Matagorda, Texas, a distance of just over 229 miles.

"Go big. Don't be stupid, but don't hold back. Everyone can respect that." —**Jesse Richman**

# LONG-BOARDING

is a form of skateboarding in which the skateboard is both longer and wider than a regular board.

**AKA** sidewalk surfing

# BEGINNINGS

LONGBOARDS DEVELOPED FOR riders to have more stability on big hills and be able to achieve greater speed. They're also popular as a means to get around since they're cheaper than a bike and much easier to store.

# BOARDS

## SHORTER BOARDS

Boards from 27 inches to 36 inches are more agile for carving and turning.

## LONGER BOARDS

Boards from 36 inches to 48 inches are more stable for gaining speed on downhill runs.

## HYBRID BOARDS

Boards around 40 inches provide some of the benefits of both shorter and longer ones.

# STYLES

## DOWNHILL RACING

Riders go as fast as possible on a downhill run getting low on the board in curves to keep it under control.

## SLALOM

Riders weave around cones or objects going as fast as they can as a test of carving skills.

## FREERIDING

Riders maneuver the board for slides or get it in the air for flip tricks like shove-its and ollies.

# COMPETITIONS

NATIONAL LONGBOARD competitions are held in countries around the world. In addition, World Cup Races bring longboarders from different nationalities together to determine who is the best in the world. Recent World Cup Races have been held in Argentina, Brazil, Colombia, and Italy.

"Injuries may come with what I love to do. But what also comes with it is thrill, competition, excitement. I have found a hidden talent, and I will not stop because of some scratches. It lets me escape. It is my anti-drug. It is longboarding."

**—Ryan A. Villa**

# MOTOCROSS

involves racing motorcycles on off-road courses. The word is a combination of *motocyclette*, the French word for motorcycle, and the English word *cross-country*.

**AKA** moto X, freestyle moto X

# BEGINNINGS

MOTOCROSS BEGAN IN the United Kingdom, with cross-country races on motorcycles over 100 years ago.

The Scottish Six Days Trial in July 1909 developed as one of the most challenging motorcycle races in the world. It ran from Edinburgh to John O'Groats, Scotland, a distance of over 250 miles. This race has been held each year since with the exception of cancellations during the two world wars.

In the 1980s, American riders caught up to European riders and motocross races began to be held on courses in large arenas.

In 1999, freestyle motocross gained popularity after being introduced at the X Games. The new emphasis on acrobatic stunts in the air rather than racing represented a major shift in the sport.

# STARS

CAREY HART IS famous for being the first person to perform the invert seat grab with feet straight in the air at the Gravity Games in 1999. This trick is now known as the Hart Attack.

Mike Metzger won the Big Air and Freestyle events at the 2002 X Games. He topped it off by completing a backflip over the fountains at Caesars Palace and landing 125 feet away from the ramp.

In 2004, Brian Deegan became the first person to execute a 360, an off-axis backflip, in competition. He called it the "Mulisha Twist."

Travis Pastrana was the youngest X Games gold medal winner at 15 and is the inventor of many freestyle motocross tricks, including a double backflip, which he landed at the 2006 X Games.

> "It scared me to death. It just doesn't make sense. You're still on your motorcycle at the height of the jump, going "this thing's not going to rotate around." I knew it was possible. It just didn't seem logical."
>
> **—Travis Pastrana**

# MOUNTAIN BIKING

is off-road bicycling over difficult terrain using specifically designed mountain bikes that are tougher and more durable than regular bikes.

AKA **MTB**

# BEGINNINGS

IN 1896, THE United States Army experimented with using bicycles off-road. The Buffalo Soldiers Bicycle Corps, a regiment of African American soldiers, pedaled from Fort Missoula, Montana, to Yellowstone in Wyoming and back. They also made the 1,900-mile journey from Fort Missoula to St. Louis, Missouri.

Even though people had been modifying bikes and riding them on mountain trails, it wasn't until the 1970s that companies began to make bikes specifically for mountain biking.

# STYLES

### DOWNHILL
Riders ride their bikes down a steep hill as fast as they can.

### DIRT JUMPING
Riders ride bikes on dirt tracks with jumps and do tricks in midair.

### FREE RIDING
This includes everything from downhill racing to performing tricks in the air in a combination of all the elements of the sport.

# SPEED DEMON

MARKUS STÖCKL HOLDS a couple of incredible speed records. In 2011, he reached 102 miles per hour while racing down the side of a volcano at Cerro Negro in Nicaragua. In 2007, he raced down snow at a ski slope at La Parva, Chile, and set a record of over 130 miles per hour.

# DISTANCE RECORD

DAVE BUCHANAN RODE 48 hours on a mountain bike in May 2011. He biked from Cardiff to Caernarfon in the United Kingdom, a distance of just over 354 miles. Seventy percent of the distance was off-road, which he said helped keep him awake and focused.

# BAD CRASH

IN 2009, ÉRIC BARONE reached record speeds of 106 miles per hour at Cerro Negro in Nicaragua before his bike frame came apart. He flew off the bike and suffered five broken ribs and a dislocated shoulder.

# RECOVERY

ÉRIC VOWED NEVER to race at Cerro Negro again, but he came back from his crash to set a new record of 138 miles per hour on snow at Les Arcs, a ski resort in France.

# MOUNTAIN BOARDING

uses a special type of rugged skateboard to ride on dirt, grass, or gravel.

AKA dirt boarding, off-road boarding, and all-terrain boarding (ATB)

# BEGINNINGS

IN THE 1990s, snowboarders looking for ways to practice without snow rigged up homemade boards and began going down the grass of ski hills in the summer.

In 1992, Jason Lee, who developed the term *mountain boarding*, founded MountainBoardSports with Patrick McConnell and Joel Lee to build boards specifically designed for mountain boarding.

In the 1990s, individuals in Australia, France, and the United Kingdom also developed boards that could be ridden on different surfaces.

## STYLES

### BOARDERCROSS
Teams of two or four members fight for position as they race through turns and fly over jumps on dirt courses.

### DOWNHILL
Riders speed down a long mountain course trying to get the best time. Riders can achieve speeds of over 50 miles per hour on these runs.

### FREESTYLE
Riders use ramps and jumps in terrain parks to get big air and perform tricks and maneuvers.

# GEAR

MOUNTAIN BOARDERS USUALLY wear protective gear. Helmets, wrist guards, elbow pads, and knee pads are helpful in case of falls or crashes.

## EXTRA DANGER

JASON LEE SET the record for the longest mountain board backflip when he jumped 29 feet and 3 inches. To make it more dangerous, he made his jump over a pit of 500-pound alligators.

"The nice thing is that with the board you ride anywhere you want so the whole planet is open." —**Jason Lee**

# MOUNTAIN CLIMBING

consists of scaling mountains and coming back down. Some climbers achieve record speeds, find new routes, or climb without using ropes as guides.

**AKA** mountaineering, skyrunning

# BEGINNINGS

FOR THOUSANDS OF years, people have climbed mountains for adventure, in search of food, to avoid enemies, or to undertake religious pilgrimages.

One of the earliest climbers on record is Ötzi, the Iceman. He reached a height of 10,530 feet in the Alps. He did this over 5,000 years ago, and his remains were found preserved as a mummy inside a glacier.

Mountain climbing became a well-known sport in the eighteenth and nineteenth centuries. Climbers competed to scale unclimbed mountains, such as Mount Everest, the highest mountain on Earth, at 29,029 feet. Edmund Hillary of New Zealand and Tenzing Norgay of Nepal reached the summit on May 29, 1953.

In the twenty-first century, after all the summits had been climbed, the emphasis shifted to faster climbs, more difficult routes, and going solo or with less equipment.

"I have been seriously afraid at times but have used my fear as a stimulating factor rather than allowing it to paralyze me. My abilities have not been outstanding, but I have had sufficient strength and determination to meet my challenges and have usually managed to succeed with them."
**—Edmund Hillary**

# CLIMBING STAR

UELI STECK OF Switzerland, who's known as the "Swiss Machine," holds a number of speed records for difficult climbs. On February 13, 2008, he climbed the north face of the Eiger—a climb that takes many people two days—in 2 hours and 47 minutes. A year later, on January 13, 2009, he climbed the north face of the Matterhorn in 1 hour and 56 minutes to set another record. Steck, who trains year-round, often climbs dangerous routes with no ropes to guard against a fall.

"Climbing the steep, exposed sections is not the dangerous part because there you are moving slowly, making sure each hold is good. The dangerous part is when you are running up the slopes because there you are moving fast. If you trip or slip, you are done."
**—Ueli Steck**

# PARAGLIDING

**involves sitting in a harness and flying lightweight, nonmotorized gliders that have hollow fabric wings.**

# STYLES

### PARAGLIDING

Regular paragliding equipment is so compact that it can be stored in a backpack, which makes it easy to carry.

### PARASKIING

Paraskiers attach skis and then ski down remote mountain runs. They lift up and glide over rocks and obstacles before resuming skiing.

### POWERED PARAGLIDING

With a small engine attached, powered paragliders can sail longer distances such as across the Grand Canyon.

# INCREDIBLE RACE

THE RED BULL X-Alps race, which crosses the Alps Mountains from east to west, is one of the most intense races in the world. For the 2013 race from Salzburg, Austria, to Monaco, athletes hiked, climbed, and paraglided over 1,500 miles in a striking display of endurance and determination.

In the first race, held in 2003, seventeen athletes started out, but only three made it to the finish line. The winner was Kaspar Henry of Switzerland who finished in 11 days and 23 hours.

The race permits each athlete a two-person support team to provide logistics and communication and requires that athletes rest between 10:30 p.m. and 5:00 a.m. In 2013, for the first time, each athlete was allowed one "Night Pass" to hike, but not paraglide, during the night.

The 2013 race was won by Christian Mauer of Switzerland, who also won it in 2009 and 2011. He flew 1,422 miles and hiked 166 in a record time of 7 days, 1 hour, and 23 minutes. He beat his nearest competitor by 180 miles.

# NEVER TOO OLD

IN 2007, PEGGY McAlpine claimed the record for oldest person to paraglide tandem when she was 100.

Her record was broken by Mary Allen Hardison when she was 101.

So in 2012, when she was 104, Peggy McAlpine paraglided tandem again to regain her world record.

# PARKOUR

is a training method in which participants called traceurs run, jump, vault, roll, and climb over obstacles getting from one point to another.

**AKA PK**

# BEGINNINGS

**A**S LONG AS people have been moving, they've overcome obstacles and challenged themselves to get places as quickly as possible.

The French military developed a training program called *parcours du combattant* that emphasized getting from one point to another efficiently and safely.

David Belle heard about this training from his father, Raymond Belle, who had adapted it for himself with extra running, jumping, and climbing. David learned these techniques and practiced with his friend Sébastien Foucan in the 1980s and modern parkour was born.

Sébastien Foucan went on to develop free running, which shares many similarities with parkour but places a greater emphasis on style and self-expression.

# GEAR

**N**OTHING IS NEEDED for parkour other than regular clothes and a good pair of shoes.

# QUOTES FROM DAVID BELLE

"Many people open their mind through different things like music and painting, as well as parkour. How is not important. What is important is to open your mind because you gain some freedom through it."

"When you're training parkour with passion, if you're good, people will notice you. Don't go around saying, 'Hey look at this new move I got.' No. We used to say, 'If it's good we'll tell you.' Do it for yourself first."

"First, do it. Second, do it well. Third, do it well and fast—that means you're a professional."

"My thing from the beginning is to have it be useful, and be able to help others. It's about being efficient and getting there as fast as you can. If people want to do it more artistically or in a freestyle way, I have absolutely no problem with it—that's the way it's going to evolve. It's not my style, but if it's other people's, that's perfect."

# ROCK CLIMBING

involves climbing up and down rock formations or on artificial climbing walls.

# BEGINNINGS

**P**EOPLE HAVE BEEN climbing rocks as long as they've lived near them in search of food, for protection, or as tests of strength.

# STYLES

### FREE CLIMBING

Climbers use their own strength and rely on ropes and other equipment purely for safety.

### BOULDERING

Bouldering is a form of free climbing over short distances of natural or artificial surfaces with a crash pad or bouldering mat underneath to cushion any falls.

### FREE SOLO

Climbers climb by themselves without using ropes or any system of protection other than their own skill and ability. This is the most dangerous form of rock climbing and a fall can result in death.

# SKILLS

**P**HYSICAL STRENGTH, BALANCE, flexibility, and endurance are all important in rock climbing, but climbers emphasize that the most important skill is mental strength, being able to make good decisions about what's possible.

# BASIC TIPS

- Keep your arms straight while hanging in place.
- When you get stuck, move your feet.
- In the beginning, try to keep three parts of your body in contact with the rock or wall.

# LOCATIONS

**R**OCK CLIMBING DOES not require mountains. States across the country have good places to climb. Climbing gyms and Web sites can direct you to those that fit your level of skill and experience.

# BROTHERLY STARS

**I**KER AND ENEKO Pou are rock-climbing brothers from Spain who are famous for their bold wall and alpine climbs.

"Success is not about standing at the top. It's the steps you leave behind."

—Iker Pou

# SAND-BOARDING

consists of riding down a sand dune on a board. It's similar to snowboarding but takes place on sand instead of snow.

## BEGINNINGS

SOME REPORTS INDICATE that early Egyptians in the time of the pharaohs slid down desert sand dunes on pieces of wood.

In the 1980s, sandboarding developed in Southern California through the efforts of Jack Smith and Gary Fluitt.

Sandboarding is now a worldwide sport with tournaments in Australia, Brazil, Chile, Dubai, Egypt, Germany, and Namibia.

## BOARD TYPES

### TWIN TIPS
These boards have identical turned-up tips that allow movement in either direction.

### SQUARE TAILS
These are designed for speed and stability when the rider is going in one direction.

### SWALLOW TAILS
These boards have a V-shaped gap cut out of the tail end and are designed for quick turns.

"The more you sandboard, the better it gets. It's a sport where you get to have fun and get a workout at the same time. It's great to be part of something so new."
**—Josh Tenge**

## FIRST AMERICAN PARK

SAND MASTER PARK in Florence, Oregon, is the first dedicated private sandboarding park. It contains 40 acres of sand dunes with beginner to advanced slopes as well as rail slides and jump ramps. It's also the site every July of the Sand Master Jam competition.

## RECORDS

ERIK AXL JOHNSON, an American sandboarder and snowboarder, holds the sandboard speed record at 51 miles per hour.

Josh Tenge, an American sandboarding champion, set the record for the longest distance on a backflip at 44 feet and 10 inches.

# SKATE-BOARDING

is the sport of riding and performing tricks on a skateboard.

# BEGINNINGS

SKATEBOARDING BEGAN AS a way for surfers to practice when waves weren't good, and one of the original names for skateboarding was sidewalk surfing.

In the 1960s, skateboards were manufactured using clay or metal wheels, the same type of wheels that were used for roller skates.

The introduction of polyurethane wheels in the 1970s revolutionized skateboarding. These wheels gripped the surface better and resulted in a boom in popularity for the sport.

In 1975, the Del Mar National Championships in California featured a clash between the traditional upright skating style and a new low-to-the-ground style represented by the Zephyr Skate Team, which was heavily influenced by Hawai'ian surfing. These skaters, known as the Z-Boys, fundamentally changed the way people skated.

California experienced a severe drought in 1976 and many swimming pools were drained. Skaters used these pools to practice climbing the vertical walls, introducing the importance of vert tricks to skating. In 1976, the country's first two skate parks, Skateboard City in Florida and Carlsbad Skatepark in California, opened ushering in a new boom in skating.

By 2001, more kids in America skated than played baseball.

# STANCES

## REGULAR
Skating with your left foot forward

## GOOFY
Skating with your right foot forward

## SWITCH STANCE
Switching from your preferred style

## NO STANCE
Some skaters, such as Rodney Mullen, experiment with not having a dominant stance.

"I love the fact that there is now a skate park in almost every city, but it will always have a rebellious/underground edge because it is based on individuality."
**—Tony Hawk**

"The body follows the mind. You keep it true, keep it true to your heart, and everything comes together."

**—Tony Alva**

# SKIM-BOARDING

involves riding a skimboard,
which is smaller than a
surfboard and does not have fins,
to glide across the water.

# BEGINNINGS

SKIMBOARDING BEGAN AT Laguna Beach in Southern California in the 1920s when lifeguards used pieces of wood to move across shallow water along the beach.

In the 1970s, skimboarding gained attention with the focus on Laguna Beach and riders such as Tex Haines and Peter Prietto.

# STYLES

## FLATLAND

Flatland skimming, also known as inland skimming, doesn't require ocean waves so it's possible away from the coasts. The shores of lakes, ponds, quarries, and channels all can work as sites for flatland skimming.

## WAVE

Wave skimming is done at the ocean using waves that break near the shore. Skimboarders begin at the beach and run across the sand and skim out to breaking waves, which they catch to ride back to shore.

# BOARD TYPES

## CRUISER

The slope on a cruiser board is slightly pointed at the top and slightly rounder in the back.

## TRICK

On trick boards, both sides are symmetrical and the shape is even throughout, making it easier to reverse direction.

# THE VIC

LAGUNA BEACH IS the site each summer of the Vic, the longest running contest in skimboarding. Since 1976, skimboarders from around the world have competed for prizes at the birthplace of skimboarding.

# OTHER GOOD SKIMBOARDING SITES

- Cabo San Lucas, Mexico
- Dewey Beach, Delaware
- Santa Cruz, California
- Many sites in Florida

"Skimboarding has given me a whole lot, particularly things like self-esteem, confidence, being able to set a goal and accomplish it." **—Paulo Prietto**

# SKYDIVING

**consists of people jumping out of airplanes singly, paired, or in groups. Skydivers free-fall until they open their parachutes.**

## BEGINNINGS

IN 1797, IN Paris, France, André-Jacques Garnerin jumped from his balloon at 8,000 feet. He floated to earth using a silk parachute attached to a basket in which he sat.

In 1914, Georgia Broadwick, who was nicknamed "Tiny" because she was 5 feet tall and weighed 85 pounds, demonstrated parachuting to the United States Army. After a jump where her static line tangled in the tail of the aircraft, she cut the line on her next jump and deployed her chute herself during free fall.

## SPEED

FREE FALL CAN last between 50 to 80 seconds and jumpers may reach speeds of up to 130 miles per hour. They can reduce the speed by opening their bodies wide to create more wind resistance.

Once skydivers reach top speed, they no longer sense the acceleration, but instead feel like they are floating.

## DANGER

EVEN THOUGH JUMPING out of a plane seems dangerous, skydiving is safer than many other extreme sports with less than one death for every 150,000 jumps.

## STRANGE RECORD

ACTOR AND FORMER Power Ranger Jason David Frank holds the record for most 1-inch pine boards broken during a free fall. While his partners, who were also free-falling, held the boards, Jason punched through seven boards during a jump on January 17, 2013.

## UNBELIEVABLE SPEED

ON OCTOBER 14, 2012, Felix Baumgartner jumped out of a balloon that was floating 24 miles above the New Mexico desert. During his almost six-minute free fall, he reached a top speed of over 833 miles per hour, or mach 1.24, which is faster than the speed of sound. He became the first man ever to break the sound barrier during free fall.

"When I was standing there on top of the world, you become so humble. You don't think about breaking records anymore, you don't think about gaining scientific data—the only thing that you want is to come back alive." **—Felix Baumgartner**

# SKY SURFING

is a form of skydiving in which riders imitate surfing maneuvers during free fall with a board attached to their feet. They open their parachutes and remove the board as they approach the ground. Advanced sky surfers can do loops, rolls, and helicopter spins.

# BEGINNINGS

IN THE 1980s, California skydivers began experimenting with jumping out of planes with Styrofoam boogie boards.

In 1986, two French skydivers, Dominique Jacquet and Jean-Pascal Oron, invented what they called the sky surf.

Sky surfing gained exposure in the 1990s as it was a prominent sport at the X Games and was featured in major television commercials.

# BOARDS

THE BOARDS USED are usually smaller than a regular surfboard and are closer in size to a snowboard.

# TEAMWORK

SKY SURFING OFTEN uses two-person teams. One person performs various moves and the other one films him using a helmet-mounted camera.

# DANGER

ADDING A BOARD to skydiving makes balance much trickier and sky surfers have to guard against the possibility of suddenly flipping over.

Because of the complexity, sky surfers should have at least 200 parachute jumps before they begin sky surfing.

A number of sky-surfing stars had accidents that claimed their lives, including Patrick de Gayardon, Vic Pappadato, Jerry Loftis, and Rob Harris. Harris, who was 28, died while making a Mountain Dew commercial on December 14, 1995.

# CHALLENGES

SKY SURFING WAS dropped from the X Games after 2000. Because of a shortage of instructors, the dangers of flying and releasing the board, and competition from BASE jumping, freeflying, and wingsuit flying, it has declined in popularity.

# SLACKLINING

involves moving across a line
that is attached to two fixed
points, often trees. The line has
more give than a traditional
tightrope and allows athletes to
try jumps, twists, and flips.

# BEGINNINGS

ROPE WALKING HAS been around for centuries, but it's usually done with a rope that's strung tightly.

Modern slacklining began in 1979 when Adam Grosowsky and Jeff Ellington, students at the Evergreen State College in Olympia, Washington, who were rock climbers, experimented with walking on one-inch climbing webbing.

The sport initially developed among rock climbers but became popular with a wide variety of people.

# STYLES

## TRICKLINING

Performing tricks on a slackline that is set up at low, medium, or high heights

## HIGHLINING

Slacklining at high elevation above the ground or water

## WATERLINING

Slacklining over water with the line set up high above the water, close to the surface, or even underwater

# COMPETITIONS

THE WORLD SLACKLINE Federation was formed in 2011 to promote slacklining. It supports tricklining competitions with emphasis on difficulty, diversity, performance, and technique. Competitions are held in Austria, Brazil, France, Germany, the United Kingdom, and the United States.

# EXPOSURE

ANDY LEWIS BROUGHT greater exposure to slacklining when he was featured during the Super Bowl halftime show in 2012.

"Living in the moment, being immersed in the wilderness, challenging your body, developing your mind, confronting, controlling, and conquering one's fear of death, and pursuing the pure, true, and honest unbridled feeling of freedom to do what you want is the foundation supporting the Slacklife."

**—Andy Lewis**

# SNOW-BOARDING

uses a special board on which athletes ride, jump, race, and perform tricks on snow.

# BEGINNINGS

**P**EOPLE WHO LIVE in cold climates have experimented with riding boards on snow for years by standing up when going downhill or being pulled by a horse.

Modern snowboarding began in 1965 when Sherman Poppen of Michigan fastened two skis together and called his invention the snurfer, a combination of the words *snow* and *surfer*.

In 1979, the first national snurfing championship was held in Muskegon, Michigan, and Jack Burton Carpenter of Vermont showed up with a snowboard he'd designed.

In 1983, the first world championship snowboarding halfpipe competition was held in Soda Springs, California.

# HUGE GROWTH

**I**N 1985, ONLY 7 percent of United States ski areas allowed snowboarding. Today, over 97 percent do. Snowboarding has been an Olympic sport since 1998.

# STYLES

## ALPINE
In what's also known as free-carving, riders compete carving on groomed runs.

## BIG AIR
Riders perform tricks after going off jumps.

## FREERIDE
Riders use the terrain to execute a wide variety of snowboarding moves.

## HALFPIPE
Riders demonstrate tricks while going from one side to the other and getting air.

## RACING
Riders compete on a downhill course while navigating gates.

## SLOPESTYLE
Riders generate tricks while maneuvering through a course filled with obstacles.

"What does it mean to be a snowboarder? It's about having fun, with your friends or by yourself. It's about pushing yourself to try new things and do the unexpected. Finally, and most importantly, it's about being creative." **—Shaun White**

"Embrace the mountain on its own terms."

**—Travis "Trice" Rice**

# SNOWMOBILING

**consists of drivers racing, jumping, and doing tricks while riding specially designed snowmobiles.**

## BEGINNINGS

EVER SINCE COMMERCIALLY manufactured snowmobiles became available in the 1950s, riders have tested the limits of speed, jumping, and maneuverability.

As machines became lighter in the 2000s, snowmobilers could jump farther, opening up the possibility for new tricks and flips.

## STYLES

### BOONDOCKING

Riders create their own trails through the woods and swamps.

### FREESTYLE

Athletes ride off jumps and do tricks in the air while holding on to the snowmobile before landing.

### MOUNTAIN CLIMBING

Riders compete in extreme hill climbing, sometimes in backcountry locations without marked trails.

### SNOWCROSS

Riders race high-performance snowmobiles on specially made tracks with sharp turns and jumps.

## RECORD JUMP

ON JANUARY 1, 2012, champion snowmobiler Levi LaVallee established a new world record with a jump of 412.5 feet at Scotts Valley, California. This was over 50 feet longer than the previous record, which he also held.

## LEVI'S INJURIES

A PARTIAL LIST of Levi's injuries includes separations to both shoulders, a dislocated wrist, a broken heel, compartment syndrome of the calf, and multiple concussions.

## TRAGEDY

ON JANUARY 24, 2013, Caleb Moore came up short as he tried to land a backflip at the X Games in Aspen, Colorado. His snowmobile bounced on top of him causing severe injuries. He died a week later, the first person to die from injuries suffered during the X Games.

"Work your tail off, stay positive, and have fun." —Levi LaVallee

# STAND UP PADDLE SURFING

involves a rider standing upright on a board and using a paddle to move through the water or into the surf.

**AKA** SUP, stand up paddle boarding, *Ku Hoe He'e Nalu* in Hawai'ian

## BEGINNINGS

STANDING UPRIGHT ON a board and paddling is an ancient activity with roots in Polynesian culture.

Modern paddle surfing began in the 1960s when surfing instructors in Hawai'i used the technique to position themselves for taking pictures and as an alternative activity when the surf was low.

The sport spread from Hawai'i to California through the support of surfers Laird Hamilton, Dave Kalama, and Rick Thomas and then to the rest of the country since it can be done on lakes, large rivers, and canals.

## ADVANTAGES OF SUP

- By being higher up in the water, the paddler can see more.
- Athletes of all abilities can be involved.
- It's easy to learn with most people being able to get on the board after a short lesson.
- By working the arms, legs, core, and upper body, it's a great form of cross-training.
- It provides the feeling of walking on water.

"The world doesn't need more conformists. If you don't fit in, celebrate that, and then get ready to stand your ground."
**—Laird Hamilton**

## COMPETITION

STAND UP PADDLE surfing has its own world championship series, the Stand Up World Tour. It was established in 2009 and athletes from different countries compete in events in California, Hawai'i, Brazil, France, and Abu Dhabi. Judging criteria include using the paddle as a necessary aid for riding the waves.

## GROWING PAINS

AS PARTICIPANTS IN a newer sport, stand up paddlers have been criticized at beaches and online from more established surfers. Stand-up paddlers emphasize that they have as much right to the waves as anybody and surfing and other water sports have always prized individuality.

# SURFING

consists of a surfer standing on a surfboard riding waves and performing a variety of twists, turns, and tricks.

# BEGINNINGS

POLYNESIAN PEOPLE HAVE been surfing for centuries using a variety of different-sized boards.

Traditional Hawai'ians placed a major emphasis on *he'e nalu*, which translates as "wave sliding," what we now know as surfing.

In 1912, Duke Kahanamoku, an Olympic swimmer, brought surfing from Hawai'i to California and Australia. He is considered the father of modern surfing.

Surfing's popularity exploded in the 1960s with television shows, films, and music groups identifying with the surfing scene.

# BOARDS

## SHORTBOARDS

These are 6 to 7 feet in length with a pointed nose and a roundish or squarish tail. They have between 2 to 5 fins on the bottom to provide increased maneuverability.

## LONGBOARDS

These are large single-finned boards with a rounded nose that range from 8 to 14 feet. Longboards allow beginners and established surfers to catch waves more easily.

## FUN BOARDS

These are usually 6 to 8 feet long and combine elements of short and longboards. They are more maneuverable than longboards and easier to catch waves on than shortboards.

# TOW-IN SURFING

IN THE 1990s, surfers began using Jet Skis to tow them into waves that were too difficult to paddle into. In the 2000s, some surfers began using helicopters with an attached towline to reach gigantic waves.

# HUGE WAVES

THE UNIQUE GEOGRAPHY of Nazaré, Portugal, allows for some incredible waves. Garrett McNamara of Hawai'i continues to break his own big-wave records, and in January 2013 claimed to have surfed a 100-foot wave.

"The joy of surfing is so many things combined, from the physical exertion of it, to the challenge of it, to the mental side of the sport."

—Kelly Slater

# WAKE-BOARDING

involves riding a wakeboard on water while being towed by motorboat. Wakeboarders move in and out of the wake and use ramps for jumps and sliders for rails.

# BEGINNINGS

IN THE 1980s, Jeff Darby and friends in Queensland, Australia, made their own skurf boards. "Skurf" is a combination of the words *water skiing* and *surf*.

In the United States in 1983, Howard Jacobs experimented with attaching windsurfing foot straps to small surfboards in Florida.

In the 1990s, new wakeboards hit the market that were lighter and stronger, which allowed for easier starts and expanded the sport.

# BASIC JUMPS

## ROLL

The rider rolls edge over edge on the wide side of the board in the air like he's doing a side somersault.

## FLIP

The rider flips the narrow, tail end of the board over the nose in the air like he's doing a cartwheel.

# STYLES

## BIG AIR

Riders go off a jump or kicker and demonstrate rolls and flips while trying to get as much air as possible.

## BOAT

While being pulled by a boat, riders hit the wake to get air to perform a variety of tricks.

## RAIL RIDING

Riders are pulled by a cable through a park and create new ways to enter, exit, and ride rails.

# CAREER CHANGE

KEITH LYMAN, WHO reached his dream of becoming a champion wakeboarder, announced that he was going to step away from the sport to achieve another one of his dreams—that of joining the military. He enlisted to serve his country in 2011.

"Inspiration comes from so many different things, good water conditions, a sunset session, who is in the boat, how big the wake is. . . . I am continually seeking new and different ways to become inspired. Sometimes it comes so easily, and other times it's a struggle."

**—Keith Lyman**

# WAVESKI SURFING

is a cross between kayaking and surfing in which riders paddle in the surf while riding in waveskis. Riders maneuver their waveskis and attempt aerials, flip aerials, and other tricks.

# BEGINNINGS

IN THE 1970s, Danny Broadhurst of New York created an early version of the waveski, though it was heavy and difficult to operate.

In the 1980s, the sport became more popular in Australia, France, Spain, the United Kingdom, and the United States.

In the 2000s, waveskis became lighter, stronger, and more durable. These changes allowed riders greater flexibility as they experimented with new moves.

# FIN ADJUSTMENT

## FORWARD
With the fins in the forward position, carves can be tight in radius, allowing surfing in small waves.

## BACK
With fins in the backward position, carves can be longer and riders will have more hold in powerful waves.

# JUDGING CRITERIA

WAVESKI COMPETITIONS ARE held around the world and some of the judging criteria are similar to other surf sports.

- The waveski surfer must perform committed, radical maneuvers in the most critical sections of a wave with style, power, and speed to maximize scoring potential.
- Innovative and progressive surfing will be taken into account when awarding points.
- The waveski surfer who executes this criteria with the highest degree of difficulty and control on the better waves shall be rewarded with the highest score.

# WAVESKI VERSUS SURF SKI

## WAVESKI
The rider sits on top of a short, curved waveski with foot straps. He paddles into the surf for tight turns and aerials.

## SURF SKI
The rider sits in the cockpit of a long, narrow kayak that is ideal for speed, but difficult to turn quickly. Surf skis are often used in surf lifesaving competitions.

# WHITEWATER
# KAYAKING

consists of paddling a kayak on rapids, fast-moving water, or over waterfalls.

# BEGINNINGS

**P**EOPLE HAVE BEEN paddling canoes and kayaks on whitewater for thousands of years. Portaging around rapids is time consuming so the temptation to run rapids when possible is strong.

In the 1970s, Tom Johnson designed the first Hollowform kayaks. Made of polyethylene, these were much more durable than previous boats. Their indestructibility meant paddlers could now bounce off rocks, opening up many new rivers and streams.

# STYLES

### FREESTYLE

Freestyle kayaking, also known as playboating or rodeo, emphasizes staying in one place in the river where riders work with the flow of the water and perform loops, spins, flips, cartwheels, and other tricks.

### RIVER RUNNING

River running focuses on going down a river from one point to another in the most direct and stylish way. As kayakers have become more daring about taking on whitewater, this can include running slides, ledges, and waterfalls.

### SLALOM

In slalom events, kayakers compete in timed heats while moving through a course of gates. Green gates are passed through while going downriver and red gates while going upriver.

### The International Scale of River Difficulty

| | |
|---|---|
| Class l | Easy small waves |
| Class ll | Medium moderate waves |
| Class lll | Difficult high, irregular waves |
| Class IV | Very Difficult high waves with dangerous rocks |
| Class V | Extremely Difficult long, violent rapids with long drops |
| Class Vl | Formerly U for Unrunnable extremely dangerous, possibly deadly |

# BEING FIRST

**A** SMALL GROUP of kayakers compete to be the first ones to descend a particular stretch of whitewater. Steve Fisher, the three-time world champion, has made over 100 first descents.

# HUGE WATERFALLS

**E**XTREME KAYAKERS ARE going over higher and higher waterfalls, and a few riders have plunged straight down from 100-foot drops.

# WINDSURFING

involves jumping, looping, and spinning while riding on a board with a sail attached to it. Windsurfing combines elements of surfing and sailing in a new way.

**AKA** sailboarding, boardsailing

# BEGINNINGS

POLYNESIAN PEOPLE HAVE been riding waves using a solid board with a vertical sail for thousands of years.

In 1965, S. Newman Darby wrote a promotional article for *Popular Science* magazine about his invention that he called a sailboard.

Windsurfing became popular in the 1980s to such an extent that it became an Olympic sport in 1984.

In the 1990s, a strong rivalry developed between windsurfers and kitesurfers that persists even though many athletes now participate in both sports.

# STYLES

### FORMULA

Formula riders use a shorter and wider board that can be turned for a wide range of wind conditions as they engage in competitive course racing.

### FREESTYLE

In freestyle, riders attempt jumps, tricks, and transitions in timed competitions. They are judged on technical performance as well as energy, diversity, and the overall fluidity of the run.

### WAVE

Wave competitions are similar to freestyle competitions but take place in ocean surf. Competitors are scored on jumps on waves going out as well as wave rides coming in.

# BIG SURF

SOME WINDSURFERS CHASE storms in order to go out in windy conditions to ride the biggest waves that they can find.

# DISTANCE RECORD

THE LONGEST WINDSURFING journey took place from May 17 to July 18, 2005, when Flavio Jardim and Diogo Guerreiro traveled from Chui to Oiapoque, Brazil, a distance of 5,045 miles.

"For me every day on the water is a good day. No matter how I get out there, it's good to get on the ocean." **—Robby Naish**

# WINGSUIT FLYING

consists of a flyer wearing a specially designed wingsuit jumping off an object or cliff or out of a plane, zooming through the air, and then deploying a parachute as he nears the ground.

# BEGINNINGS

MAN HAS DREAMED of flying for generations. In Greek mythology, Icarus attempted to escape from Crete using a suit of wings and wax that his father made. Icarus ignored his father's instructions and flew too close to the sun. His wings melted and he fell into the sea and drowned.

In 1930, Rex Finney of California and others made wingsuits out of canvas, wool, silk, and steel. These early wingsuits were not very reliable.

In the late 1990s and 2000s, major technological advances led to more sophisticated wingsuits and the number of participants increased dramatically.

# THE SUIT

REGULAR WINGSUITS HAVE three wings between the arms and legs while mono-wing suits encompass the whole body. These inflate and form an airfoil that provides lift and enables gliding. The suits have been described as resembling birds, bats, flying squirrels, or superheroes.

# STRENGTH

FLYING A WINGSUIT takes strength to use it to full capacity. Using advanced techniques, riders can slow to 40 miles per hour or less, which allows more time to make maneuvers.

# SPEED

WINGSUIT SPEEDS AVERAGE around 100 miles per hour, but riders can reach speeds of over 150 miles per hour depending on wind conditions.

# DANGER

BECAUSE OF THE speed and the proximity to natural objects like rocks and cliffs, wingsuit flyers must make very quick decisions. A wrong decision by the flyer frequently results in death.

# RECORDS

ON MAY 28, 2011, Shin Ito of Japan set the record for fastest speed reached in a wingsuit at 226 miles per hour.

"People who've seen me about to fly off a cliff say I look perfectly calm. It's the complete opposite. I'm terrified. I've just developed techniques and methods to cope with the fear." —**Espen Fadnes**

THE FIRST X Games, which were called the Extreme Games, were held in 1995 in Newport, Rhode Island. They were created by ESPN as a way to attract younger viewers to ESPN and its partner network ABC, both divi-sions of The Walt Disney Corporation. Few people realized what a profound impact these games would have on the world of sports. The initial games included bungee jumping, aggressive inline skating, mountain biking, skate-boarding, sky surfing, and street luging. They were so successful that ESPN decided to make them an annual event rather than hold them every two years.

Some extreme-sport ath-letes didn't want to have any-thing to do with an organized competition sponsored by a major corporation. They thought such an event violated the alternative spirit of their sport and that the participants were being used to sell products to kids. They also thought that this type of structured event seemed too much like traditional sports. But other athletes jumped at the opportunity to highlight their talents and make some money and find sponsors. They wanted to get paid for doing what they loved.

In 1997, the first winter X Games took place in Big Bear Lake, California, featuring snowboarding, ice climbing, snow-mountain-bike racing, and super-modified shovel racing. The winter X Games were broadcast to 198 countries in 21 languages. The pattern was then set for the winter games to be held each year in January or February and the summer games to be held in June, July, or August.

In 1997, the summer X Games shifted to San Diego, California, for two years before going up the coast to San Francisco for 1999 and 2000. They moved back east to Philadelphia, Pennsylvania, for 2001 and 2002. After that, the summer X Games located to Los Angeles, where they got bigger every year from 2003 to 2013 before they shifted to Austin, Texas, in 2014.

The winter X Games moved to Crested Butte, Colorado, for 1998 and 1999, adding events in snowcross, freeskiing, and snowmobiling. After two years, the games shifted back across the country to Mount Snow, Vermont, for 2000 and 2001. In 2002, they moved to Aspen, Colorado, with slopestyle and superpipe added to the skiing events. The winter X Games have been held each year in Aspen ever since.

The X Games expanded to Asia in 1998 with a competition in Thailand and to Europe in 2010 with a major event in France. In 2013, the X Games held contests in four cities outside the United States: Tignes, France; Foz do Iguaçu, Brazil; Barcelona, Spain; and Munich, Germany. After that, they decided to focus on the games in the United States.

By broadcasting live coverage of skiing, snowboarding, and snowmobiling in the winter and BMX, motocross, mountain biking, and skateboarding in summer, the X Games introduced these sports to a wider audience and gave kids a chance to see their favorite athletes compete against one another. Stars such as Shaun White, Travis Pastrana, Tony Hawk, Bob Burnquist, Mat Hoffman, and Dave Mirra won multiple gold medals at the X Games and gained many new fans.

In 1999, at X Games 5, Tony Hawk landed the first 900, two and a half revolutions, on his skateboard. The pattern of athletes trying out their newest and coolest tricks has been a feature of the X Games since. All kinds of amazing things have happened at the X Games, which is one of the reasons so many people across the world tune in—to see something that's never been done before.

# FIRST-TIME TRICKS AT X GAMES

THE X GAMES are an ideal place for athletes to showcase new feats that they've been working on. In 2013, Mitchie Brusco, who was 16, landed a 1080, three full revolutions on his skateboard, at the summer X Games. Afterward he said, "I figured there was no better place to do it than here. I mean all the big stuff goes down at the X Games."

Most of these amazing first-time tricks at the X Games can be viewed online. Even years later, many require multiple viewings to figure out how they were done.

# FIRST-TIME TRICKS at WINTER ✖ GAMES

- In 2001, Mike Jones performs the Kiss of Death in Moto X Best Trick. While inverted, he kicks his feet in the air as he hangs on to the handlebars of his bike.
- In 2004, Caleb Wyatt wins Moto X Best Trick with a no-handed backflip over a 90-foot gap.
- In 2007, Peter Olenick completes the first double flip—the whiskey flip—in halfpipe competition in Ski Superpipe.

- In 2011, Torstein Horgmo performs the first triple cork in Snowboard Big Air.
- In 2012, Heath Frisby nails the first snowmobile front flip in Snowmobile Best Trick.
- In 2013, Torstein Horgmo pulls off the first switch triple cork 1440 to win Snowboard Big Air.
- In 2013, Iouri "iPod" Podladtchikov completes the first cab double cork 1440 in the Snowboard

Superpipe. He calls it the YOLO Flip.
- In 2013, Heath Frisby lands the first underflip in Snowmobile Best Trick.
- In 2013, Henrik Harlaut performs the first-ever nose butter triple cork 1620 to win the Ski Big Air.
- In 2013, Joe Parsons nails the Gator Hater, a snowmobile flip where he lands facing backward on the seat of his sled in Snowmobile Best Trick.

# FIRST-TIME TRICKS at

# SUMMER

# GAMES

- In 1999, Tony Hawk lands a 900, two and half revolutions, on his skateboard.
- In 2000, Dave Mirra does the first-ever double backflip in the BMX Park competition.
- In 2001, Taïg Khris performs the first double backflip in Inline Aggressive Skating Vert.
- In 2001, Danny Harf pulls off a 900 in the wakeboarding competition.
- In 2002, Mat Hoffman lands a no-handed 900 in BMX Vert.
- In 2002, Mike Metzger nails back-to-back backflips in Moto X Freestyle.
- In 2003, Brian Deegan performs the first ever 360 in Moto X Freestyle.
- In 2004, Chuck Carothers wins Moto X Best Trick with the Carolla. He extends his legs behind him while holding the seat and then twists around to land back on his bike.
- In 2005, Jamie Bestwick lands the first-ever double tail-whip flair in the BMX Vert Best Trick event.
- In 2006, Travis Pastrana sticks the first double backflip on a dirt bike in freestyle Moto X.
- In 2006, Kevin Robinson demonstrates the first double flair in BMX Vert Best Trick.
- In 2007, Simon Tabron pulls off the first back-to-back 900s in BMX Vert.
- In 2009, Anthony Napolitan performs a double front flip in the BMX competition.
- In 2011, Jackson Strong nails a front flip in the Moto X Best Trick competition.
- In 2012, at the Asia X Games, 12-year-old skateboarder Tom Schaar lands the first 1080 in competition on the Mini Mega ramp.
- In 2013, Jake Brown lands the first ollie 720 in Skateboard Big Air.
- In 2013, 16-year-old Mitchie Brusco pulls off the first 1080 on the MegaRamp during Skateboard Big Air.

# BOB "BIG BOB" BURNQUIST

BOB "BIG BOB" BURNQUIST, the skateboarder, has won more X Games medals than any other athlete. He was born in Rio de Janeiro, Brazil, and grew up skating in São Paulo. He's known for his ability to skate equally well in regular or goofy stance, which makes more combinations possible. One of his most extraordinary X Games performances came in the Vert competition of 2001. He was in second place before his final run, but he produced an amazing series of tricks, including many that had never been seen before, for a score of 98, which allowed him to win gold.

# TANNER HALL

TANNER HALL IS one of the most successful and influential free-skiers of all time. He was born in Kalispell, Montana, and grew up skiing at Whitefish Mountain Resort. He's won X Games medals in Big Air, Slopestyle, and Halfpipe and was the first person to three-peat in Halfpipe. He's returned to competition twice after serious injuries. In 2005, he broke both ankles in a fall and, in 2009, he broke both legs and two ACLs. Tanner Hall is also an outspoken advocate for keeping freestyle skiing "real."

# TONY "THE BIRDMAN" HAWK

TONY "THE BIRDMAN" HAWK grew up in San Diego, California, started skating when he was 9, and turned pro when he was 14. He brought the X Games to a new level on June 27, 1999, when he became the first person to successfully land a 900, something he'd been working on for years. He retired from competition after winning fourteen X Games medals, but continues to perform in exhibitions and to be a major spokesman for the sport. He's also established the Tony Hawk Foundation, an organization that builds skate parks in low-income areas around the country.

# MAT "THE CONDOR" HOFFMAN

MAT "THE CONDOR" HOFFMAN was born in Edmond, Oklahoma, and as a boy dreamed of flying. He got his first BMX bike when he was 11 and turned pro when he was 17. By becoming a champion in BMX Freestyle in his teens, he was able to realize his flying dreams. In the 2002 X Games, he stunned the crowd when he pulled off a no-handed 900 to win BMX Vert. Over the years, he's come back from more than sixty broken bones and over twenty surgeries. He's a major contributor to growing the sport of BMX riding.

# MIKE "THE GODFATHER" METZGER

MIKE "THE GODFATHER" METZGER is one of the innovators
in freestyle motocross. He was born in Huntington Beach, California, and by 4, he was jumping off a ramp on his Big Wheel. At
6, he raced on his dirt bike on the track his father built behind
their house. In the 2002 X Games, he won the freestyle gold
medal by performing back-to-back backflips, a trick he called the
Double Fritz in honor of his dad and grandfather. He also won
the silver medal in Step Up and another gold in Big Air, when
he executed a backflip while taking his hands off the handlebars
while upside down.

# DAVE "MIRACLE BOY" MIRRA

DAVE "MIRACLE BOY" MIRRA won medals in every X Games from 1995 to 2008, and currently holds the record for second most X Games medals. He was born in Chittenango, New York, and started riding BMX bikes with his brother when he was 5. He turned pro when he was 18, but his career nearly ended when he was hit by a drunk driver when he was 19. Despite concerns that he might not ride again, he came back to win fourteen X Games gold medals in BMX Park, Street, and Vert. He now lives in Greenville, North Carolina, a major center of the BMX world.

# SHAUN "PALM DADDY" PALMER

SHAUN "PALM DADDY" PALMER is one of the most versatile athletes in X Games history. He won gold medals in four different sports: snow mountain bike racing, snowboard cross, ski cross, and ultracross. He was born in South Lake Tahoe, California, and from an early age was interested in extreme sports. As an X Games champion, he brings an aggressive style and an intense desire to win. In addition to competing in all these sports, he was the lead singer in the punk band Fungus.

# TRAVIS "WONDER BOY" PASTRANA

TRAVIS "WONDER BOY" PASTRANA is an X Games champion in multiple sports who continues to push himself. He was born in Annapolis, Maryland, and by age 4 he was riding a Honda one-speed. At the X Games in 1999, he won the first-ever Moto X Freestyle with the incredible score of 99 points. In 2006, he landed the first double backflip in competition and won three gold medals in Rally, Moto X Freestyle, and Moto X Best Trick. In addition to his X Games success, he also races in NASCAR and promotes interest in all the sports in which he's involved.

# GARRETT REYNOLDS

GARRETT REYNOLDS HAD an amazing run of six straight gold medal wins (a six-peat) at the X Games in BMX Street. In 2013, in Los Angeles, he stormed back in his final run, but lost by one point to Chad Kerley. Afterward, Garrett said, "It's an honor to be beat by that guy." Garrett was born in Toms River, New Jersey, and became a pro at 13. Despite being one of the best street riders of his generation, he's known for being modest, humble, and supportive of other riders.

# SHAUN "THE FLYING TOMATO" WHITE

SHAUN WHITE SOARS at the X Games on his snowboard in the winter and on his skateboard in the summer. He was born in San Diego, California, with a heart defect and had two major surgeries before he was 1 year old. He was skiing by 4 and started snowboarding at 6. In 2011, he became the first person to win gold medals in the winter and summer X Games in the same year. Shaun currently holds the X Games record for the most gold medals. He also performs with his band Bad Things and is active with St. Jude Children's Research Hospital, Boys and Girls Clubs, Target House, Make-A-Wish Foundation, and Stand Up for Skateparks.

OTHER

COMPET

IN ADDITION TO the X Games, other events and competitions sprang up to highlight athletes and their sports. The Gravity Games, which were developed originally in partnership with NBC Sports, ran from 1999 to 2006 and featured aggressive inline skating, skateboarding, BMX freestyle, wakeboarding, freestyle motocross, and snowboarding.

The Dew Tour is named for Mountain Dew, a division of PepsiCo, which was one of the first major companies to link its products with extreme sports. The tour showcases sports in three categories: a beach championship in June, a city championship in October,

and a mountain championship in December. Alli Sports, a division of NBC Sports, organizes the events, and NBC broadcasts them through various platforms. The Dew Tour includes BMX events in Park, Vert, and Street, skateboarding events in Vert, Bowl, and Street, and snowboarding Slopestyle and Superpipe.

Red Bull, the energy drink company, is a major sponsor of extreme sports. The company, headquartered in Austria, supports competitions around the world in cliff diving, windsurfing, mountain biking, free running, paragliding, and freestyle motocross. One of the Red Bull events Crashed Ice involves

TIONS

groups of skaters racing down a steep sheet of ice with jumps and sharp turns. As the name indicates, crashes occur frequently. In addition to its own competitions, Red Bull sponsors many high-profile athletes in different sports.

Other companies, like Vans, which sponsors the Vans Pro Skate Tour, and Nike, which is involved with the Street League Skateboarding Super Crown World Championships, have made significant investments. Makers of skateboards, surfboards, and other gear sponsored early competitions and athletes, and this has continued as skaters, surfers, and other athletes create their own companies. Today, there are hundreds of events, tours, and competitions for extreme sports from the ones small enough to fit in a parking lot to others that fill gigantic arenas.

"You know the best thing about competition? There's this whole strategy game, and when it all works out it's like solving that hard math equation. You finally get the answer and you're so happy." **—Shaun White, snowboarder and skateboarder**

# THE
# OLYMPICS

ONE OF THE biggest indicators of the worldwide reach of extreme sports is their inclusion in the Olympic Games. This began in 1984 when men's windsurfing, under the names boardsailing and wind gliding, became a medal sport at the Los Angeles Games. This exposure increased interest and windsurfing has remained part of the Summer Olympics ever since.

For the Winter Olympics, 1992 was a significant year. Freestyle skiing moguls became a medal sport and aerials were a demonstration sport in Albertville, France. Edgar Grospiron of France won the gold medal in moguls, much to the delight of the French fans. His countryman Olivier Allamand won silver and American Nelson Carmichael won bronze. In 1994, aerials were added as a medal sport in Lillehammer, Norway, bringing freestyle skiing to a much wider audience.

In 1996, cross-country mountain biking debuted as a medal sport at the Summer Games in Atlanta. Bart Brentjens of the Netherlands won the first gold medal and mountain biking has remained part of the Olympics since. In 1998, snowboarding became a medal sport in the halfpipe and giant slalom competitions at the Winter Games in Nagano, Japan. Ross Powers of the United States won the bronze medal in halfpipe, and snowboarding became one of the most popular events.

Four years later, in the 2002 Winter Olympics in Salt Lake City, parallel giant slalom, with two racers racing side by side, replaced giant slalom as a medal event in snowboarding. In halfpipe, with home-country fans cheering them on, American riders swept the medal round with Ross Powers, Danny Kass, and Jarret Thomas winning gold, silver, and bronze.

In 2006, at the Winter Olympics in

Turin, Italy, snowboard cross, in which four riders race down the course against one another, debuted as a medal sport, joining halfpipe and parallel slalom. It proved a crowd-pleasing addition and has remained a medal sport since then.

For the Summer Olympics, the next important advance occurred in 2008 in Beijing, China. BMX racing became a medal sport and Americans Mike Day and Donny Robinson won silver and bronze medals. Television had brought BMX racing to a much larger global audience and it became an Olympic hit.

In 2010, at the Winter Olympics in Vancouver, Canada, ski cross was added as a medal sport. It joined moguls and aerials to become the third freestyle-skiing event. For the 2014 Winter Olympics in Sochi, Russia, three new events were added. Slopestyle was added as a medal competition in both snowboarding and skiing, and halfpipe was added in skiing as well. There are now five medal sports in freestyle skiing and four in snowboarding.

Even with the addition of these sports to the Olympics, there's room for more. If snowboarding has four different medal competitions, one question leaps to mind. Where's skateboarding? The Summer Olympic Committee is hesitant to increase the total number of athletes. So when a sport is added, something else must go. Guess which sport got dropped from the Summer Olympics in London in 2012?

Baseball was eliminated. What a sign of the shift in interest when baseball is no longer part of the Summer Olympics and windsurfing, mountain biking, and BMX racing are. Which sports do you think should be added to the Olympic Games? Which ones do you think should be dropped to make room for those new ones?

# OLYMPIC

# MEDALS

WHEN YOU THINK OF FREE-style skiing and snowboarding at the Winter Olympics and BMX, mountain biking, and windsurfing at the Summer Olympics, which athletes do you think have won the most medals? Which countries do you think have dominated the medal count? Take a look at the medal winners and see how correct you are.

# WINTER

## MOGULS

| GAMES | GOLD | SILVER | BRONZE |
|---|---|---|---|
| 1992 Albertville | Edgar Grospiron<br>France | Olivier Allamand<br>France | Nelson Carmichael<br>USA |
| 1994 Lillehammer | Jean-Luc Brassard<br>Canada | Sergey Shupletsov<br>Russia | Edgar Grospiron<br>France |
| 1998 Nagano | Jonny Moseley<br>USA | Janne Lahtela<br>Finland | Sami Mustonen<br>Finland |
| 2002 Salt Lake City | Janne Lahtela<br>Finland | Travis Mayer<br>USA | Richard Gay<br>France |
| 2006 Turin | Dale Begg-Smith<br>Australia | Mikko Ronkainen<br>Finland | Toby Dawson<br>USA |
| 2010 Vancouver | Alexandre Bilodeau<br>Canada | Dale Begg-Smith<br>Australia | Bryon Wilson<br>USA |
| 2014 Sochi | Alexandre Bilodeau<br>Canada | Mikaël Kingsbury<br>Canada | Alexandr Smyshlyaev<br>Russia |

## AERIALS

| GAMES | GOLD | SILVER | BRONZE |
|---|---|---|---|
| 1994 Lillehammer | Andreas Schönbächler<br>Switzerland | Philippe LaRoche<br>Canada | Lloyd Langlois<br>Canada |
| 1998 Nagano | Eric Bergoust<br>USA | Sébastien Foucras<br>France | Dmitri Dashinski<br>Belarus |
| 2002 Salt Lake City | Aleš Valenta<br>Czech Republic | Joe Pack<br>USA | Aleksei Grishin<br>Belarus |
| 2006 Turin | Han Xiaopeng<br>China | Dmitri Dashinski<br>Belarus | Vladimir Lebedev<br>Russia |
| 2010 Vancouver | Aleksei Grishin<br>Belarus | Jeret Peterson<br>USA | Liu Zhongqing<br>China |
| 2014 Sochi | Anton Kushnir Belarus<br>Belarus | David Morris<br>Australia | Jia Zongyang<br>China |

# OLYMPICS

## MEN'S FREESTYLE SKIING

### SKI CROSS

| GAMES | GOLD | SILVER | BRONZE |
|-------|------|--------|--------|
| 2010 Vancouver | Michael Schmid Switzerland | Andreas Matt Austria | Audun Grønvold Norway |
| 2014 Sochi | Jean-Frédéric Chapuis France | Arnaud Bovolenta France | Jonathan Midol France |

### SLOPESTYLE

| GAMES | GOLD | SILVER | BRONZE |
|-------|------|--------|--------|
| 2014 Sochi | Joss Christensen USA | Gus Kenworthy USA | Nick Goepper USA |

### HALFPIPE

| GAMES | GOLD | SILVER | BRONZE |
|-------|------|--------|--------|
| 2014 Sochi | David Wise USA | Mike Riddle Canada | Kevin Rolland France |

# WINTER

## HALFPIPE

| GAMES | GOLD | SILVER | BRONZE |
| --- | --- | --- | --- |
| 1998 Nagano | Gian Simmen<br>Switzerland | Daniel Franck<br>Norway | Ross Powers<br>USA |
| 2002 Salt Lake City | Ross Powers<br>USA | Danny Kass<br>USA | Jarret Thomas<br>USA |
| 2006 Turin | Shaun White<br>USA | Danny Kass<br>USA | Markku Koski<br>Finland |
| 2010 Vancouver | Shaun White<br>USA | Peetu Piiroinen<br>Finland | Scotty Lago<br>USA |
| 2014 Sochi | Iouri Podladtchikov<br>Switzerland | Ayumu Hirano<br>Japan | Taku Hiraoka<br>Japan |

## GIANT SLALOM

| GAMES | GOLD | SILVER | BRONZE |
| --- | --- | --- | --- |
| 1998 Nagano | Ross Rebagliati<br>Canada | Thomas Prugger<br>Italy | Ueli Kestenholz<br>Switzerland |

## PARALLEL GIANT SLALOM

| GAMES | GOLD | SILVER | BRONZE |
| --- | --- | --- | --- |
| 2002 Salt Lake City | Philipp Schoch<br>Switzerland | Richard Richardsson<br>Sweden | Chris Klug<br>USA |
| 2006 Turin | Philipp Schoch<br>Switzerland | Simon Schoch<br>Switzerland | Siegfried Grabner<br>Austria |
| 2010 Vancouver | Jasey-Jay Anderson<br>Canada | Benjamin Karl<br>Austria | Mathieu Bozzetto<br>France |
| 2014 Sochi | Vic Wild<br>Russia | Nevin Galmarini<br>Switzerland | Žan Košir<br>Slovenia |

# OLYMPICS

## MEN'S SNOWBOARDING

### PARALLEL SLALOM

| GAMES | GOLD | SILVER | BRONZE |
|---|---|---|---|
| 2014 Sochi | Vic Wild<br>Russia | Žan Košir<br>Slovenia | Benjamin Karl<br>Austria |

### SLOPESTYLE

| GAMES | GOLD | SILVER | BRONZE |
|---|---|---|---|
| 2014 Sochi | Sage Kostenburg<br>USA | Ståle Sandbech<br>Norway | Mark McMorris<br>Canada |

### SNOWBOARD CROSS

| GAMES | GOLD | SILVER | BRONZE |
|---|---|---|---|
| 2006 Turin | Seth Wescott<br>USA | Radoslav Židek<br>Slovakia | Paul-Henri de Le Rue<br>France |
| 2010 Vancouver | Seth Wescott<br>USA | Mike Robertson<br>Canada | Tony Ramoin<br>France |
| 2014 Sochi | Pierre Vaultier<br>France | Nikolay Olyunin<br>Russia | Alex Deibold<br>USA |

# SUMMER

## MEN'S WINDSURFING

| GAMES | GOLD | SILVER | BRONZE |
|---|---|---|---|
| 1984 Los Angeles | Stephan van den Berg<br>Netherlands | Scott Steele<br>USA | Bruce Kendall<br>New Zealand |
| 1988 Seoul | Bruce Kendall<br>New Zealand | Jan Boersma<br>Netherlands Antilles | Mike Gebhardt<br>USA |
| 1992 Barcelona | Franck David<br>France | Mike Gebhardt<br>USA | Lars Kleppich<br>Australia |
| 1996 Atlanta | Nikolaos Kaklamanakis<br>Greece | Carlos Espínola<br>Argentina | Gal Fridman<br>Israel |
| 2000 Sydney | Christoph Sieber<br>Austria | Carlos Espínola<br>Argentina | Aaron McIntosh<br>New Zealand |
| 2004 Athens | Gal Fridman<br>Israel | Nikolaos Kaklamanakis<br>Greece | Nick Dempsey<br>Great Britain |
| 2008 Beijing | Tom Ashley<br>New Zealand | Julien Bontemps<br>France | Shahar Tzuberi<br>Israel |
| 2012 London | Dorian van Rijsselberghe<br>Netherlands | Nick Dempsey<br>Great Britain | Przemysław Miarczyński<br>Poland |

# OLYMPICS

# MEN'S MOUNTAIN BIKING

| GAMES | GOLD | SILVER | BRONZE |
| --- | --- | --- | --- |
| 1996 Atlanta | Bart Brentjens<br>Netherlands | Thomas Frischknecht<br>Switzerland | Miguel Martinez<br>France |
| 2000 Sydney | Miguel Martinez<br>France | Filip Meirhaeghe<br>Belgium | Christoph Sauser<br>Switzerland |
| 2004 Athens | Julien Absalon<br>France | José Antonio Hermida<br>Spain | Bart Brentjens<br>Netherlands |
| 2008 Beijing | Julien Absalon<br>France | Jean-Christophe Péraud<br>France | Nino Schurter<br>Switzerland |
| 2012 London | Jaroslav Kulhavý<br>Czech Republic | Nino Schurter<br>Switzerland | Marco Aurelio Fontana<br>Italy |

# BMX

| GAMES | GOLD | SILVER | BRONZE |
| --- | --- | --- | --- |
| 2008 Beijing | Māris Štrombergs<br>Latvia | Mike Day<br>USA | Donny Robinson<br>USA |
| 2012 London | Māris Štrombergs<br>Latvia | Sam Willoughby<br>Australia | Carlos Oquendo<br>Colombia |

# DE

## "IF YOU DI

ONE OF THE fundamental rules of extreme sports is that you must survive to tell the stories of your accomplishments. From the beginning, the stakes have been high in sports where a sudden shift in weather, an equipment malfunction, or one bad decision can result in death.

Rob Harris was the world champion of sky surfing in 1994 and 1995. Because of his skills, PepsiCo invited him to participate in a Mountain Dew commercial. For the filming, Rob dressed up in a tuxedo to portray a James Bond–type hero escaping from an exploding airplane. Rob and his partner, Joe Jennings, filmed multiple takes over a few days. But on December 14, 1995, the lines of one of Rob's parachutes got tangled up and his reserve chute didn't open

in time. He crashed to the ground and died instantly. He was 28 years old. PepsiCo representatives asked Rob's parents about running the commercial, which contained the previous shots. After some hesitation his parents agreed since they believed Rob would have wanted this. The commercial is available on YouTube as a memory of Rob and his life.

On January 24, 2013, snowmobiler Caleb Moore soared 100 feet into the air for a backflip at the X Games. He came up short and his skis caught the lip of the landing. Caleb flew forward over the handlebars onto the snow. Unfortunately, his 450-pound snowmobile rolled over the top of him. He lay on the ground for a while before getting up and walking off as millions of people watched on live

# TH
# YOU LOSE."

television. He was taken to a hospital, but he died a week later from his injuries. Caleb was 25. A family spokesman said, "He lived his life to the fullest. He was an inspiration."

Athletes in a wide range of extreme sports have died while pursuing their passions. Tyrone Gilks, Eigo Sato, and X Games champion Jeremy Lusk all died in freestyle motocross crashes. Ice climber Dave Church was killed in a 75-foot fall and Jack Roberts was killed in a 60-foot fall. Wingsuit pioneer Patrick de Gayardon, X Game champion camera flyer Vic Pappadato, and sky-surfing innovator Jerry Loftis all died in separate accidents in the same year. Mario Richard participated in 7,000 skydives and 2,000 BASE jumps and said he'd never suffered even

a sprained ankle. But he died in Italy on August 19, 2013, when he hit a cliff wall while BASE jumping.

Even a sport like kayaking, which is not considered one of the most dangerous, can be deadly. Kayaker Jeff Ellis was killed after he went over a 15-foot waterfall and was pulled back toward the falls as his kayak took on water. He was unable to execute an Eskimo roll, and the kayakers he was with weren't able to save him. In 2010, Hendrik Coetzee, an experienced kayaker, paddled along the Lukuga River in the Democratic Republic of Congo. He was in between two other kayakers when a 15-foot crocodile weighing around a ton rose out of the water, snatched him out of his kayak, and pulled him underwater. His remains were never found.

ON MARCH 13, 2012, snowboarder Nickolay Dodov and his helicopter ski guide Rob Liberman died in an avalanche in Alaska. Ben Clark, the director of a documentary about the tragedy called *The Alaskan Way*, poses a question on a blackened screen.

*Is living the dream worth risking it all?*

Many extreme-sport athletes would quickly answer yes. Some would say that to die doing what they love is exactly what they want. But this quick answer ignores those who are left behind when a young athlete dies.

Ben Clark, who climbed Mount Everest and participated in extreme skiing and rock climbing, interviewed both Nickolay Dodov's and Rob Liberman's parents for *The Alaskan Way*. He reacted strongly to their grief. He remembered a confrontation he'd had with his own parents over his decision to quit his job to climb Mount Everest and reflected back on it.

"It had nothing to do with dying, doing something you love, or being willing to risk your life for something that thrills you. People think that's admirable. But the people who think that's admirable were not the people that were close to me, that I loved, that I left behind. We need to let people know that it's not just about you and the risk you take, it's about what you leave behind when you make this decision."

In *The Crash Reel*, director Lucy Walker explores the intense competition in snowboarding between Shaun White and Kevin Pearce leading up to the Winter Olympics in 2010. On the morning of December 31, 2009, Kevin dropped into a halfpipe in Park City, Utah, to attempt a double cork trick—three and a half rotations with two and a half inverted spins. It was something he'd been struggling with but knew he needed to master for the Olympics. He caught an edge coming out of the spins and slammed into the pipe so fast he didn't have time to get his hands in front of his face.

*The Crash Reel* follows Kevin's long and difficult recovery from wiggling a finger after twenty-six days to his decision to return to snowboarding. But that decision is not without complications since he's suffered a severe brain injury and his doctor warns him that another blow to his head could be catastrophic. Still, Kevin Pearce wants to return to the sport he loves and the film includes a powerful scene where he tells his family he's 100 percent confident about that. Kevin's brother David, who has Down syndrome, expresses his feelings about Kevin's decision.

"I don't want you to die, that's one, and then number two is that I don't want you to be in a wheelchair and I don't want you to be paralyzed. Is that what you want?"

"That's not what I want," Kevin says. "I think those are all things that I could have happen if I fall."

*The Crash Reel* dramatically explores the tension between an elite athlete who wants to return to competition and his family who wants him to stay alive. In the documentary, Kevin Pearce underwent the journey of figuring out who he is and what he wants. He is now a television commentator, motivational speaker, and advocate for brain injury and Down syndrome research. He was selected as one of the torch carriers at the 2014 Winter Olympic Games in Sochi, Russia, and is the founder of LOVEYOURBRAIN, an organization focused on brain injury prevention, rehabilitation, and health.

MIKE SCHULTZ WAS born and grew up in Kimball, Minnesota. He started racing motocross in 1997 and snowcross in 1998. He competed in snow-cross in six winter X Games. In December 2008, he suffered a severe accident while racing. He broke his leg so badly that it had to be amputated above the left knee. Mike was back riding his sled within a month. He now wins gold medals in both Adaptive Motocross and Adaptive Snowcross in the X Games, using the Moto Knee, a prosthetic he helped develop.

Mike's Web site is monstermikeschultz.com.

### WHEN DID YOU START RACING?

My first competitive event was actually on a BMX bike when I was 13. I did that for two years and then had my first motocross race when I was 15. The first motocross race started off a bit rough after I got run over by a few bikes in the first corner but fortunately I wasn't injured so I popped back up and kept on going. Since then I've been hooked on racing. A couple of years after that I started racing snowmobiles in the winter season and dirt bikes in the summer. The season of 2001–2002 is when I signed my first contract with a snowmobile race team to race semi-pro. In 2003–2004, I moved up into the pro class and was racing with the best guys in the world. I was living my dream as a pro racer!

### WHAT DID YOU THINK ABOUT RACING AFTER YOUR THREE SURGERIES IN 2008?

I had been injured many times and have always recovered. So, when the doctors told me that amputating my leg was the best thing in order for me to survive, it was a fairly easy decision. But at that point I was sure my racing days were over. My mind-set changed and I started to take one day at time and focused on the recovery much like any other injury.

### MANY ATHLETES HAVE SUFFERED BROKEN LEGS. DID IT SEEM UNFAIR THAT YOUR BREAK WAS SO SEVERE?

At no point did I ever ask "Why did this happen to me?" I understood that severe injuries were always a possibility. I hoped and thought it would never happen, but it did and now I had to deal with the consequence of having a high-risk occupation. I was definitely bummed out about the situation and how I thought it was going to change my life. But instead of looking at the things I couldn't do, I focused on the things I could.

### HOW DID YOU GET INTO DEVELOPING PROSTHETIC DEVICES AND WHO ELSE IS

# S T I O N S

## F O R

# "MONSTER MIKE" SCHULTZ

### BENEFITING FROM MOTO KNEE?

Once I physically recovered and started walking on my prosthetic leg five and half weeks after the accident, I started to understand and learn how the equipment worked but soon realized that even the best equipment wouldn't get me back on the bike or snowmobile. Those activities have been my focus and livelihood for a long time and I wanted to keep doing it, maybe not racing but just for fun. I am the type of guy who looks at a machine or piece of equipment and tries to figure out how to make it better, so of course I wanted to build myself a "riding leg." This really got going when I heard of the ESPN Summer X Games Adaptive Motocross, which is a dirt-bike race for amputees and paraplegics. I thought to myself, I have to be part of this! That's when I started working on my own leg in my shop and soon had a prototype that utilized a FOX Air Shock coupled with a linkage system that I developed to make it feel like my real leg. It worked very well right from the beginning, and seven months after my accident in July 2009, I was at the Summer X Games Adaptive Motocross race. I ended up taking the silver medal! During that summer, I also realized that other amputee athletes could benefit from my design. In the summer of 2010, I started my company called Biodapt, Inc., which manufactures the leg I developed, the Moto Knee. I have customers around the world using it for sports such as snowboarding, skiing, wakeboarding, horseback riding, and ATV, motorcycle, and snowmobile racing. Not long after my accident I made the decision that I was going to make something good come out of this life-changing event, and after a lot of hard work, dedication, and support from my family and friends, I now have a very rewarding job that is helping others enjoy some of the fun activities in life.

### WHAT ADVICE DO YOU HAVE FOR YOUNG RACERS?

If you truly want to be a successful racer, you need to understand that dedication and preparation are everything. You get out of racing what you put into it. The harder you practice and train during the week, the better your results will be on race day. If you don't put the effort in during the week, then don't be bummed out when you don't do well on race day. Preparation means practice and training but it also means using the proper safety equipment to prevent injuries when possible and making sure your equipment is always working right and is well maintained. The best advice I can give is to control what you can and react the best you can to everything else. And sometimes bad things happen and that's just the way it is.

IN RESPONSE TO the growth of extreme sports, some alternatives have emerged whose results are strictly for laughs.

Planking, also known as the lying-down game, is the strange sport where participants lie facedown on a flat surface. Legs must remain straight with toes pointed and arms must be placed by the sides with fingers pointed. Techniques include being fully supported or having only parts of the body supported. Of course planking has a Web site (planking.me), a Facebook page, and a song. Planking spots can include rails, poles, rocks, signs, garbage cans, church pews, and anything else you can think of. The Web site also offers a warning to remember to plank SAFE!

Leisure Diving, which has been defined as parkour meets planking with a pool, is another unusual sport. Participants jump into a pool while striking a pose in a relaxed or

nonchalant manner and having their picture taken. Casual or formal clothes may be worn for an additional element and props are frequently used. Photos can be seen at leisuredive.com and you're invited to send in your own. Some leisure divers even combine it with other sports like waterskiing.

In extreme ironing, also known as EI, people take an ironing board and an iron to a remote spot and iron items of clothing.

Phil "Steam" Shaw created Extreme Ironing in England, in 1997, when he combined rock climbing and ironing. Videos of people ironing while mountain climbing, canoeing, waterskiing, skydiving, tightrope walking, and scuba diving are unlike anything you've seen. The Extreme Ironing page on Facebook offers this definition: "Extreme Ironing combines the thrill of extreme outdoor activity with the satisfaction of a well-pressed shirt. Iron on!"

EXTREME SPORTS ARE BIG AND getting bigger. Every year more people decide that these sports that emphasize individuality, innovation, and originality are for them. What were once activities of small groups of outsiders have become a mainstream phenomenon with regularly scheduled tours, corporate sponsors, and a growing presence in the Olympics.

Even with mainstream acceptance, though, these sports continue to progress because of the creativity of individual athletes. These athletes practice for hours searching for something new. They're trying to find a way to express themselves by creating something unique. As skateboarder Rodney Mullen says:

"How do you earn respect? You earn respect by the degree to which you make yourself different. So what that does is you bring all these like-minded individuals trying to take the basic alphabet of what we do and expand it in ways that no one's ever done before, which is the inherent definition of invention."

This drive for invention is how these sports progress. Of course when you start,

you begin by imitating the tricks of others. But as you get comfortable, you find your way to create moves that express your own personality. By celebrating your individuality, like the athletes in this book do, you can create something of your own, something that nobody else has done.

If your sport is important to you, it's also necessary to work hard and take it seriously. As snowmobiler and motocross champion "Monster Mike" Schultz emphasizes, "You need to understand that dedication and preparation are everything."

Work hard. Pursue excellence. Celebrate your individuality. And don't forget those two words of advice that veteran performers offer repeatedly to extreme sports–crazy boys: Have fun!

# BIBLIOGRAPHY

## BOOKS

Brooke, Michael. *The Concrete Wave: The History of Skateboarding.* Toronto, Ontario: Warwick Press, 1999.

Browne, David. *Amped: How Big Air, Big Dollars, and a New Generation Took Sports to the Extreme.* New York: Bloomsbury, 2004.

Edwardes, Dan. *The Parkour and Freerunning Handbook.* New York: Harper-Collins Publishers, 2009.

Hamilton, Laird. *Force of Nature: Mind, Body, Soul, and, of Course, Surfing.* New York: Rodale, 2008.

Hart, Lowell. *The Snowboard Book: A Guide for All Boarders.* New York: W. W. Norton and Company, 1997.

Hawk, Tony. *Between Boardslides and Burnout: My Notes from the Road.* New York: HarperCollins Publishers, 2002.

Hoffman, Mat, with Mark Lewman. *Testimony: The Ride of My Life.* New York: HarperCollins Publishers, 2002.

Howe, Neil. *Millennials Rising: The Next Great Generation.* New York: Vintage Books, 2000.

Marcus, Ben. *The Art of Stand Up Paddling: A complete guide to SUP on Lakes, Rivers, and Oceans.* Guilford, Connecticut: Falcon Guides, 2012.

———. *Surfing USA!: An Illustrated History of the Coolest Sport of All Time.* Stillwater, Minnesota: Voyageur Press, 2005.

Mullen, Rodney, with Sean Mortimer. *The Mutt: How to Skateboard and Not Kill Yourself.* New York: HarperCollins Publishers, 2004.

Stecyk III, C. R. and Glen Friedman. *Dogtown: The Legend of the Z-Boys.* New York: Burning Flags Press, 2000.

Tomlinson, Joe, with Ed Leight. *Extreme Sports: In Search of the Ultimate Thrill.* Buffalo, New York: Firefly Books, 2004.

Warshaw, Matt. *The History of Surfing.* San Francisco: Chronicle Books, 2010.

# BIBLIOGRAPHY

## WEB SITES

aaos.org
about.com
basejumper.com
bodyboarder.com
cavediving.com
dirtragmag.com
dropzone.com
ebodyboarding.com/hubbpage
epictv.com
exploratorium.edu/skateboarding
extremesportnews.com
freeskier.com
kayaksession.com
newyorker.com
nytimes.com
olympic.org
outsideonline.com
paddlesurf.net
powder.com
pulseskimboarding.com
redbull.com/us/en/athletes
redbullstormchase.com

rockclimbing.com
sandboard.com
skateboardermag.com
skim.co
slackline.com
snowboardermag.com
surfermag.com
surfingdirt.com
surfingmagazine.com
surfline.com
teamusa.org
thrashermagazine.com
transworld.net
uswindsurfing.org
wakeworld.com
wakeboarder.com
wikipedia.org
worldrollingseries.com
xtremesport4u.com
xgames.espn.go.com
xpogo.com

Images provided by the Associated Press on pages: 125, 127, 128, 130
Images provided by Shutterstock on pages: 51, 59, 67, 69, 71, 75, 79, 83, 85, 89, 105, 115, 124, 126, 129, 131–133

# ABOUT THE AUTHOR

Skydive Dubai

**JOHN COY** is the author of picture books, young adult novels, and the popular 4 for 4 middle-grade series, which includes *Top of the Order*, *Eyes on the Goal*, *Love of the Game*, and *Take Your Best Shot*. He lives in Minneapolis and visits schools nationally and internationally. For research on this book, he participated in a number of extreme sports, including jumping out of an airplane with skydiver Junior Silva at Skydive Dubai. The view was spectacular, and yes, he would do it again.

johncoy.com

Thank you for reading this Feiwel and Friends Book.

## THE FRIENDS WHO MADE
### *FOR EXTREME SPORTS-CRAZY BOYS ONLY* POSSIBLE ARE:

**Jean Feiwel**
PUBLISHER

**Liz Szabla**
EDITOR IN CHIEF

**Rich Deas**
SENIOR CREATIVE DIRECTOR

**Holly West**
ASSOCIATE EDITOR

**Dave Barrett**
EXECUTIVE MANAGING EDITOR

**Nicole Liebowitz Moulaison**
PRODUCTION MANAGER

**Lauren A. Burniac**
EDITOR

**Anna Roberto**
ASSOCIATE EDITOR

**Christine Barcellona**
ADMINISTRATIVE ASSISTANT

Find out more about our authors and artists and our future publishing
at mackids.com.

OUR BOOKS ARE FRIENDS FOR LIFE.